The Influence of the Church on the Local Community

The Influence of the Church on the Local Community

Fruition of the Kingdom of God through Social Justice Initiatives

Abraham G. Ndung'u

Foreword by Wyndy Corbin Reuschling

WIPF & STOCK · Eugene, Oregon

THE INFLUENCE OF THE CHURCH ON THE LOCAL COMMUNITY
Fruition of the Kingdom of God through Social Justice Initiatives

Wipf & Stock
An Imprint of Wipf and Stock Publishers
199 W. 8th Ave., Suite 3
Eugene, OR 97401

www.wipfandstock.com

PAPERBACK ISBN: 978-1-7252-7348-1
HARDCOVER ISBN: 978-1-7252-7349-8
EBOOK ISBN: 978-1-7252-7350-4

01/04/21

To my parents, Naomy Njoki Ndung'u, and
the late Michael Ndung'u Wathome
for teaching me the praxis of social justice.

The place God calls you to is the place where your deep gladness and the world's deep hunger meet.

FREDERICK BUECHNER

Spirituality without morality is disembodied;
morality without spirituality is rootless.

RICHARD M. GULA

Contents

List of Tables

Foreword

Some Christian communities have created a false dichotomy between evangelism and social justice. This has tended to create false choices. One is the prioritization of evangelism while ignoring social justice or placing it lower on the moral scale of concern for other human beings. The other is a focus on justice, with little reference to how the prophets and the Gospels re-narrate God's reconciling work among persons and in communities. This created dichotomy between evangelism and social justice is convenient for us, permitting us to ignore one at the expense of the other. What we have in this book is a return to some fundamental assumptions of how we understand the kingdom of God, grounded in Scripture, guided by theological claims, informed by current work on the topic, and reflected in a particular Christian community living out their commitments in real time, real space, with real people. There are no false choices to be made as we read this book as we come to understand social justice as Gospel witness, part of God's reconciling work in our world, and a means of bringing good news to our communities.

I have been privileged to know Dr. Abraham Ndûng'û for approximately ten years, when he entered Ashland Theological Seminary where he earned two degrees. His previous work in environmental studies and urban development, his commitments as a Mennonite pastor, his reading of Scripture, his loyalty to God's kingdom, and his deep concern for God's good for all of God's creation came together in his doctor of ministry project, which you now have before you. Conversations about the relationships between the kingdom of God and the church have been ongoing and will be familiar to many readers of this book. Abraham enters into this ongoing conversation and expands it in two ways. First, he explores how this relationship between God's kingdom and the church results in, or ought to result in, an understanding of social justice as part of God's mission to reconcile a broken world. Second, rather than just leave us in this ongoing conversation about these connections between the kingdom, church, and justice, with additional scholarly resources, Abraham takes us to a particular Christian community where we observe how a church understands its mission and extends this into practices of social justice.

J. Jireh Ministries Church is located on the east side of Columbus, Ohio, in the community known as Kimball Farms: a neighborhood negatively impacted by the construction of two major interstate highways in the 1960s. Like many urban centers, these expressways, which were built for burgeoning suburban communities where money and white people were moving, devastated businesses, housing, public spaces, job opportunities, local transportation, and other social services in Kimball Farms, resulting in an impoverished, predominately African-American community. However, what did remain and still remains are God's faithful people, rooted in a community they love and has loved them, and that still witnesses by "doing justice and loving mercy" under the leadership of their pastor, Dr. Norman Brown. Abraham introduces us to this church and how they understand their mission in the various practices and programs of social justice. What is interesting are the interviews with community members, who clearly articulate how they understand what they are doing as deeply related to sharing the good news and living out the vision of the kingdom of God in tangible and reconciling ways. This community is "doing the gospel" in affordable housing projects, prison ministry, community farming, mentoring of youth, and workplace development skills, among many other things. This worshipping community shows us how social justice is an organic part of church life, with no false choices between: "Do we 'do' evangelism or do we 'do' social justice?" The answer is "Yes!"

During these turbulent days where a global pandemic has exposed the disparities, distortional, and dangerous effects on underserved communities; where African Americans receive unfair attention in policing, violent overreach in practices, more severe sentences; and where gaps in economic resources and wealth continue to widen, it is important to hear again the centrality of social justice as gospel witness in the world. Abraham has done an important service for us by introducing us to a church that has resisted the false choice between evangelism and social justice. As you read this book, may you as well find yourself answering "Yes!" to the question of whether a church is committed to evangelism or social justice. And your answer will be much stronger because of this book.

Wyndy Corbin Reuschling, PhD
Professor Emerita of Ethics and Theology
Ashland Theological Seminary
June 2020

Acknowledgments

I AM GRATEFUL TO God for his abundant grace that has enabled me to do this study. I am also thankful to my academic advisor, Dr. Wyndy Corbin Reuschling, for tirelessly guiding me through this research. Indeed, the faculty of Ashland Theological Seminary who taught me during the coursework phase of my seminary journey laid in me a firm foundation without which this dissertation work would not have been carried out.

Not to be forgotten is the keen eye of my editor, Dr. Russell Morton, and, in the early stages of the dissertation, Dr. Dawn Morton. I am sincerely grateful for all your support. I am indebted to my family for their unwavering support during my seminary journey. They put up with me during those days I was an "absent" husband and father. To all my friends, especially those of J. Jireh Ministries Church and the community of Kimball Farms, your overwhelming support is greatly appreciated.

Chapter 1

Introduction and Project Overview

I ONCE HEARD A Christian preacher say from a pulpit that he had not been called to make this world a better place in which to live. His calling, by implication, was to save souls. His mission was, therefore, to prepare souls for "shipment" from this world to heaven, their final and better destination. While this may sound funny, it represents how a number of ministries understand their mission. On a more serious note, the notion of not wanting to make this world a better place leaves many questions unanswered. Why do we seek a better life, better health, better jobs, and better livelihoods in this world if, indeed, making this world a better place is not a part of the calling of humanity, let alone Christians?

This project seeks to prove that this distorted idea about the nature of the core calling of God's people is incorrect. This project also demonstrates that the church is indeed called to a mission that goes beyond "packaging" humans for heaven, the theological ramifications of what heaven is all about notwithstanding. As Noel Castellanos has argued, the church cannot afford to perpetuate this narrow "one-dimensional gospel that is only concerned about securing people's immigration status in heaven."[1] The role of the

1. Castellanos, *Where the Cross Meets the Street*, loc. 906.

church in advancing the gospel message is much broader. This is the purpose of the present dissertation project.[2]

PURPOSE STATEMENT

It is the purpose of this project to discover how J. Jireh Ministries Church (JJMC) of Columbus, Ohio, influences the local community for the kingdom of God. The central thesis of the dissertation project can be put as follows: the mission of the church is to be God's ambassador of bearing witness to the kingdom of God. With specific reference to the geographical focus of the study, this thesis can be refined further as follows: the mission of JJMC is to be God's ambassador of bearing witness to the kingdom of God in the community of Kimball Farms in Columbus, Ohio. Thus, this project seeks to discover how effective JJMC has been in accomplishing this important role.

OVERVIEW

It is the purpose of this research project to evaluate how well JJMC has been doing in ministering to the needs of the Kimball Farms community. The study evaluates the operations of JJMC with a view to providing recommendations which, if implemented, will help improve service delivery in the local community. Implementing those recommendations will hopefully create an even greater impact for the kingdom of God.

This project began with the selection of forty potential respondents who were identified and given questionnaires to complete. These questionnaires sought information that would help to provide answers to the set research questions. The identified respondents were people associated in some way with both JJMC and the community of Kimball Farms. They were a mixture of genders and ages. The questionnaire was administered using three approaches, depending on the situation of the targeted respondent. One approach was the creation of an online internet link, where identified respondents were expected to complete the questionnaire. The second approach was to send questionnaires as email attachments. In the third approach, hard copy questionnaires were provided. After the questionnaires were completed, the researcher embarked on collating and analyzing the information gathered. Subsequently, correlations and conclusions were drawn. The culmination of all those efforts was the production of this

2. The information in the remainder of this chapter is taken from the original Research Proposal, which you can find in Appendix 1.

dissertation that answered the discovery question pivotal to this study: How has JJMC influenced its local community for the kingdom of God?

FOUNDATIONS

This research project was based on one premise: that God is, and has always been, at work in the world. The challenge, therefore, is whether humans can identify where God is at work so they can join him in what he is already doing. The kingdom of God calls for human beings to partner with God so that God's work can be accomplished. This is the case even when it is obvious that God can work without human assistance. It is, therefore, a privilege for mere mortals to join their creator in the work of the kingdom. In that regard, what JJMC is doing is an example of how God's people can be involved in his mission. That is why this research project sought to discover the extent to which this congregation is living out this mission in Columbus, Ohio, and how that is indicative of the presence of God and his kingdom in that community.

Personal Foundation

Why is this project important to me? Understanding the dynamics of the kingdom of God equips one to be an ardent promoter of stewardship and social justice education, which is an area of great need in our world today. With so many injustices around us, Christians need to speak out for the oppressed and help establish systems for promoting social justice. At the same time, Christians should challenge socio-structural systems that are an impediment to human flourishing and dignity. Christians, therefore, have no choice but to embrace the role of advocacy for and on behalf of the voiceless in society. These are some of the reasons why I undertook this study.

My involvement in Christian missions over the years has heightened my desire to see church leaders catch this same vision. Thus, the choice of this project was propelled by my desire to know what is the nature of God's kingdom and the role of the church within it. I intend to use the findings of this research project to equip other Christian leaders so they can better serve the church in fulfilling its calling. In any case, the mission of God's people is not just about calling people to Jesus Christ for forgiveness of sins. It is also about a holistic transformation of individuals, communities, and societies. The promotion of this perspective is what is intended by the results of this study and the invaluable lessons that have emerged from this work.

Biblical Foundation

The idea of the kingdom of God, which is about partnership between the creator God and humans in stewarding creation, is found both explicitly and implicitly throughout the biblical narrative. This stewardship task was given before the Fall, and humans were expected to care for the "very good" condition of the creation (Gen 1:31). This "goodness" refers to the functional rather than the moral goodness of how the cosmos operates.[3] According to Genesis 3, however, this pristine pre-Fall creation was marred by sin. Subsequently, there was need for restoration and reconciliation, the full realization of which will come in the future (see Rev 20–21). That restoration is the good news that Jesus Christ brought, and which forms the foundation of the kingdom of God (Luke 4:16–30). That is, the message of reconciliation the church has been tasked with is to bring justice in society and reconciliation of the created order to its creator God. Thus, the two passages selected for this study (2 Cor 5:16–21 and Luke 4:18–30) demonstrate that Jesus has inaugurated the long-awaited kingdom of God and that his followers have been called to be ambassadors of reconciliation. They are to propagate the message of the kingdom both in word and deed.

The church is now a signpost of that kingdom. Its mission is to point creation toward God's rule, especially in its future fulfillment. Thus, the church is to be preoccupied with the recruitment of ambassadors for proclaiming and bringing about the new creation that God has purposed with the death and resurrection of Jesus Christ. This newness, or renewal of all things (2 Cor 5:1621), constitutes the kingdom of God, which comes about through the agency of God's people. The theme of the kingdom of God is, therefore, both a continuation and a part of the grand biblical narrative about God and his people. This fact implies that one cannot discuss the subject of that kingdom outside the context of the grand narrative presented in the entire Bible. That is how the subject of the kingdom of God is associated with the concept of good news or the gospel.

Theological Foundation

Millard J. Erickson notes that the kingdom of God is neither externally imposed nor far removed. It is something present, to which human beings can enter "wherever obedience to God is found."[4] It is one which Christians are expected to spread. It is, therefore, the duty of the church to be

3. Walton, *Lost World of Genesis One*, 148.

4. Erickson, *Christian Theology*, 1163.

involved in kingdom work. This is because the church is God's ambassador of reconciliation tasked with the responsibility to carry out that kingdom work. But one very important thing ought to be unequivocally understood: kingdom-based social justice activities must not only be theistic but must, of necessity, be Christocentric. That understanding applies even in the case of socio-institutional structures involved in activities for the common good.

We cannot talk about kingdom work without mentioning a king who, in this case, is God. By extension, one cannot talk about the business of the biblical God without reference to Jesus Christ. He was God incarnate who put on humanity and lived among us (John 1:14; Phil 2:6–8). In that regard, the kingdom of God and the gospel it is associated with are about the total reconciliation of all things, humans and the entire created order, through Jesus Christ. Furthermore, Scot McKnight reminds us that the kingdom of God is not only centered around Jesus Christ, but that it is, of necessity, the business of the church.[5] It was, therefore, appropriate for this project to focus on discovering how, as ambassadors of reconciliation in God's kingdom, JJMC of Columbus, Ohio, is influencing the local community with the gospel in word and deed.

Historical Foundation

The church has historically been involved in the work of the kingdom of God, including promotion of social justice, as part of her mission in the world. It has endeavored to present the gospel holistically in word and deed by integrating social and spiritual aspects. As God's ambassadors of reconciliation, church leaders, church congregations, church institutions, and individual Christians have historically provided a prophetic voice in a society desperately in need of social justice. Those social justice-related initiatives have included advocacy as well as policy work in the public square.

In addition, Christians have been deliberately involved in promoting projects that targeted socially oppressive laws. That explains how the church has been involved in social movements whose aim was to promote human dignity and emancipation. It is within that context that some prominent individuals in the North American church have been instrumental in promoting the kingdom of God through social justice-related initiatives. Such people include Reverday C. Ransom, Charles Finney, Washington Gladden, and Martin Luther King Jr. Through such initiatives, the church has demonstrated the relevance of the gospel message by addressing challenges of life

5. McKnight, *Kingdom Conspiracy*.

that believers and non-believers face every day. Thus, the kingdom of God has become relevant in the here and now and not just in the future.

On the whole, it is noteworthy that Christians have undertaken the task of being "carriers" of the gospel message and are making a positive contribution in the world. Of course, this has not always been easygoing. However, with God's enabling power, the gospel has spread out both in word and deed to the world and to different sectors of society. JJMC is demonstrating the fact that the church is indeed tasked with the responsibility of being salt and light in society so as to bring to bear the kingdom of God.

Contemporary Foundation

Although the kingdom of God is not, and can never be, a product of human effort, it is incumbent upon humans to co-operate with God in order to realize this kingdom work. That way, God can be seen to work within human communities through Christ.[6] Disciples of Jesus Christ in particular are ambassadors of the kingdom of God. They are the salt of the earth and the light of the world (Matt 5:13–16). As God's agency for reconciling all creation to God, the church ought to be preoccupied with doing holistic ministry in the world. Thus, as the church ministers to the entire created order in order to reconcile it with the creator, Christian believers fulfill God's mandate to point society to what is right.

In that regard, a lot has been done, and is being done, to inculcate values of the kingdom into society as part of "gospelling." Numerous contemporary examples abound that indicate how the church has made this endeavor a reality through social justice-related initiatives. That is part of the church's public witness. Churches and parachurch organizations have realized the need to do social justice work that is conventionally the domain of the state and nongovernmental societies. It is encouraging to note that the church is doing this social justice work in collaboration with other stakeholders, including public-private partnerships, non-profit organizations, civil societies, and community groups. Such inclusiveness in doing social justice work is very crucial because no single individual or organization can improve society single-handedly.

The church has, therefore, recaptured the vision of addressing social justice issues as part of her mission. JJMC is an example of how churches ought to be engaged actively in the kingdom of God. This church was chosen to showcase how church in general ought to be counted on as an agency of the kingdom of God and as God's faithful ambassador of reconciliation. The

6. Niebuhr, *Christ and Culture*, 98.

church should carry out this role either singly or in partnership with other actors, such as governments and secular organizations, to address pressing social justice issues. This study is, therefore, an attempt to discover the extent to which JJMC has influenced the local community for the kingdom of God with special focus on social justice-related activities.

CONTEXT

JJMC is located in a poor neighborhood of the city of Columbus, Ohio. Residents of this area, Kimball Farms, grapple with a host of social, economic, political, and economic challenges. For example, in 2016, this locality was ranked the fourth poorest zip-code area of the city of Columbus, Ohio. Out of the thirty zip-code areas of Columbus, it scored a percentage poverty ranking level of 47.15. This is the neighborhood JJMC is called to serve and maintain a faithful witness to—in addition to ministering to its own congregants. [7]

Interestingly, this area has an awkward history. Up until recently, this neighborhood had no name, as such. It was referred to simply as "South of Main" because of its geographical location. Without a name, this neighborhood lacked identity. No wonder the area was depressed economically and socially. It was just this past year when a civic association begun by JJMC successfully petitioned to change its name from "South of Main" to "The Community of Kimball Farms." The request was granted. As I understand, this area was originally called Kimball Farms. Thus, a mere choice of a name by a civic association in recognition of the history of this neighborhood would subsequently trigger a process of healing by giving the community an identity. Ironically, other than the presence of several unused and aging grain storage silos nearby that indicate that the area might have had some farming activities, the entire area is completely urbanized. The name "Kimball Farms" is therefore a misnomer, as much as it came from the local community through an inclusive grassroots participatory process.

JJMC is actively involved in the life of the Community of Kimball Farms. That is a good reason for choosing this church for purposes of meeting the objectives of this dissertation project. This church undertakes a wide array of activities and programs within the study area (See Appendix 3). The majority of these are carried out in partnership with individuals, governmental agencies, businesses, and medical and educational institutions. The activities include weekly church services and a Bible study. The Church is

7. For the complete background of JJMC, as well as an exhaustive index of its ministries, see Appendix 3.

also involved in benevolence, visitations, prayers, and related pastoral concerns. In addition, the church conducts a number of programs like Kingdom Institute, Youth Summer Enrichment Program, and Video Game Night.

Other activities supported by JJMC are a community garden, community love feasts, community cleanups, and a national night out. The Church also convenes monthly civic association meetings; it also hosts a food pantry. It also holds community health fairs to address health and wellness as well as addressing the problem of drug and alcohol addiction. The church addresses crime and violence issues by holding peace liaison meetings in conjunction with the city's law enforcement authorities.

Unemployment matters are addressed through job fairs. There is also occasional promotion of blood donation to American Red Cross. The church addresses poor education in the area by partnering with two schools in the area, an elementary school and a middle school. The church is also involved in renovating houses for veterans in the area. Three needy groups are also ministered to: ex-offenders or restored citizens, veterans, and at-risk youth. The Church also works with other churches within the community to bring the kingdom of God to the community.

The challenge facing JJMC is how to strike a balance between ministering to the local community spiritually while meeting their physical needs. Two very important questions arise from this challenge: First, how can JJMC go beyond giving residents handouts to actually helping them to acquire life skills that would lead to self-sufficiency and independence? Second, how can this church adopt a holistic approach to ministry by linking material needs with spiritual connectedness? It is possible for this church's social programs to become a shining example of how intentional and incarnational ministries in poor urban neighborhoods ought to be run.

As indicated above, the community where this research project was conducted has myriads of issues requiring urgent attention. In this predominantly African-American neighborhood, there is human brokenness that manifests in different ways. Manifestations include domestic and gun violence, health and diet issues, unemployment, lack of self-esteem, drug abuse, broken families, low standards of education, and poor housing. This situation leads to social injustices, broken social relationships, and a lack of economic vibrancy. This ties well with Nicholas P. Wolterstorff's summary of his two experiences: his visit to the then-apartheid South Africa and his attendance at a conference in Chicago about Palestinian rights. In that regard, Wolterstorff notes that injustice is not an abstract word. It is a reality of evils meted out on real people he had met: live human beings who had been wronged, demeaned, and humiliated.[8]

The neighborhood and the general area where this project was conducted have historically experienced social and economic injustices. That has largely been a product of utilitarian-driven policy decisions that have had adverse impacts on the local community. Notable among such policies is the past decision to construct I-670, I-70, and I-71 freeways across this study area. Although these decisions were meant to promote the greatest good for the greatest number as far as economic development goes, the freeway projects actually ended up creating more harm than good for the local economy.

JJMC has therefore been working in partnership with like-minded individuals, organizations, and the local community in shaping this neighborhood by adopting holistic approaches to doing ministry. In so doing, this church has endeavored to address local injustices with a view to working out solutions that would reverse the fortunes of the residents in this area. JJMC is doing what any church congregation is expected to do: serving people indiscriminately. This research project therefore endeavors to discover what activities JJMC is involved in to bring God's holistic *shalom* into this neighborhood. In other words, the project sought to discover the extent to which JJMC has been able to practice the ministry of presence by offering a prophetic voice in a hopeless situation for the kingdom of God. In doing so, this church is able to help facilitate a restoration of justice, righteousness, and total reconciliation. Thus, as Gustavo Gutiérrez would argue, that is how ecclesial witness plays its part in addressing itself to the interplay between material poverty and spiritual poverty.[9] The two types of poverty are inseparable and, therefore, the church has no choice but to address them both in order to bring about total emancipation of the whole person. That is what JJMC is endeavoring to do.

DEFINITION OF TERMS

kingdom of God: "[T]he reign of God in human hearts wherever obedience to God is found" and which Christians are expected to spread.[10] It is God's reign dynamically active in the person of Jesus and in human history. It is present and future, inward and outward, spiritual and apocalyptic.[11]

8. Wolterstorff, *Journey toward Justice*, 7.
9. Gutiérrez, *We Drink from Our Own Wells*, 122.
10. Erickson, *Christian Theology*, 1163.
11. Ladd, *Presence of the Future*, 42.

Church: Christ's body in the world that accomplishes Christ's mission. It is a Spirit-breathed people who embody forgiveness of sins, formed by the word and sacrament around which they gather to become a *koinonia* [community] of sharing and healing. They are sent into the world to share God's forgiveness and *koinonia* with a hurting and broken world.[12] It is also "a community of humanity that experiences and communicates God's saving intentions."[13]

Missio Dei: Latin for mission of God.

Imago Dei: Latin for image of God. Humans are God's image bearers or imagers.

Shalom: The state of flourishing in all dimensions of one's existence: in relation to God, in one's relations to one's fellow human beings, in one's relation to nature, and in one's relation to oneself.[14] It is "the rich biblical image of harmonious wholeness and right relations."[15]

Social Justice: "[Having]to do with the way that material resources and social advantages are distributed and made accessible in society."[16] There is no need to narrow justice into various categories like social, economic, or even environmental justice because justice is simply justice. This is a working definition for purposes of this project and not necessarily about the narrow definition that the word "social" tends to imply.

Evangelism: Proclaiming the truths of God; living the good news of the presence of the kingdom and bringing its values into a visible, accessible, and tangible reality for others.[17]

Gospel: Good news. Something has happened as a result of which the world is a different place.[18]

PROJECT GOALS

It is the overall purpose of this project to discover how J. Jireh Ministries Church of Columbus, Ohio, influences the local community for the kingdom of God. In that regard, the specific goals guiding this project are:

12. Peterson, *Who Is the Church?*, 147.
13. Driver, *Images of the Church in Mission*, 12.
14. Wolterstorff, "Contours of Justice," 113.
15. Reuschling, *Desire for God*, 33.
16. Cannon, *Social Justice Handbook*, 31.
17. Suderman, "Reflections on Anabaptist Ecclesiology," 154.
18. Wright, *Simply Good News*, 16.

1. To discover participants' understanding of the ministries of JJMC in their community.
2. To discover the motivations of participants' involvement in JJMC.
3. To discover how participants have been personally impacted by JJMC.
4. To discover how JJMC has impacted the local community.
5. To discover how participants experience the presence of God through the presence/ministry of JJMC.
6. To discover participants' insights on important social issues in this community that need to be addressed.

DESIGN, PROCEDURE, AND ASSESSMENT

The purpose of this research project is to discover how J. Jireh Ministries Church influences the local community for the kingdom of God. The corresponding research question is: How has JJMC influenced the local community for the kingdom of God? The research design of this project is both a quantitative and qualitative study. I aim at soliciting answers to close-ended (quantitative) and open-ended (qualitative) questions. Questions are directed at respondents from the local community, both members and non-members of the congregation of JJMC.

The survey also targets community members who have been involved in the activities of JJMC in that neighborhood prior to and up to the time of the study. A questionnaire was prepared and subsequently sent out to forty potential pre-selected respondents. The questionnaire was administered using three approaches, depending on the situation of the targeted respondent. One approach was to create an online internet link where respondents were expected to complete the questionnaire. The second approach was to send questionnaires as email attachments. The third approach was to provide a hard copy of a questionnaire. All those answers were collected and collated for purposes of analysis, critical reflection, and data interpretation.

The plan was to gather survey data from local adult respondents of eighteen years of age and above. They were intentionally selected owing to their involvement with church activities in the local community. The respondents in this survey told the story of the extent to which JJMC had impacted them, their families, and other members of the local community, both directly and indirectly. Their responses contributed to the larger narrative that tells the story of how the local community had been influenced by JJMC.

This research project closely interacts with the leadership of JJMC, who provided a detailed narrative of the background of the church's presence in this community. In addition, the leaders provided information about collaborative initiatives that had been forged to address social and economic justice issues in the neighborhood. Drawing participants from within and outside the membership of JJMC helped to provide diversity and inclusiveness. This was necessary in order to discover what actual impact this Christian ministry has made in the community where it is located. The questionnaire used in the survey covered a number of issues including demographics, length of residence in the neighborhood, and church-initiated activities and practices in the neighborhood. This study was not intended to subject information collected to rigorous statistical analysis. That means there were no mathematical correlations, computations, or comparisons drawn from the data collected.

PERSONAL GOALS

The choice of a project on social justice was propelled by what I consider to be my calling. Frederick Buechner's words in his book *Wishful Thinking* appropriately express my deepest conviction regarding the need for promoting social justice: "The place God calls you to is the place where your deep gladness and the world's deep hunger meet."[19] There are four personal goals that I hoped to accomplish at the conclusion of the study:

1. To be educated on what my role is in the church as far as the kingdom of God is concerned.
2. To learn from others how to be effective in the kingdom-oriented ministry of reconciliation.
3. To be equipped to train others to be kingdom-oriented in the ministry of reconciliation.
4. To be able to launch a full-fledged kingdom-oriented ministry of reconciliation that promotes issues covered in this project.

DISSERTATION PLAN

As has been stated above, it was the purpose of this project to discover how JJMC influences the local community for the kingdom of God. Since the

19. Buechner, *Wishful Thinking*, 119.

mission of the church is to be God's ambassador of bearing witness to the kingdom of God, the focus of this project was to find out how effective JJMC has been in playing this role in the community of Kimball Farms. Given the mission of Jesus Christ, which was about the kingdom of God, the church is mandated to continue in that mission as its major reason for existence.

Thus, in a sense, this project focused on evaluating the performance of JJMC as an outpost of God's kingdom in the community of Kimball Farms. Such an appraisal is not an end in itself but a means of assessing the operations of this church. This would help generate recommendations on how to improve the local witness of JJMC with a view of making its presence more impactful. The following chapters will include biblical, theological, and historical foundations (chapter 2). The following chapter will be a review of contemporary literature (chapter 3). Next will be a detailed description of the method, procedures, and design of the project (chapter 4), and the study results (chapter 5). A final chapter (chapter 6) will reflect on the findings as they apply to Christian ministry.

Chapter 2

Biblical, Theological, and Historical Foundations

My involvement in various leadership roles both within and outside the church has enabled me to understand the importance of encouraging all people to live their lives as God intended. It is only then that we can achieve God's purpose for humanity. The objective desire for Christians to live out their faith and be effective as the light of the world and the salt of the earth (Matt 5:13–16) is in line with the overarching theme of the entire biblical narrative. The biblical story is about how God is reconciling his creation to himself, and how he invites people to accompany him in this endeavor. From a theological point of view, since reconciliation with God's creation is God's own mission, God's people are expected to carry out this task on behalf of God. Historically, the church has been involved in this task over the centuries, and there are valuable lessons that can be drawn on how this task has been accomplished. In that regard, JJMC is a test study for such endeavors.

BIBLICAL FOUNDATION

Although the two passages chosen for this study are not explicitly about the kingdom of God and social justice, the subject is nevertheless implied. In 2

Cor 5:16–21, the writer describes the mission of the church as a *kingdom community* and ambassadors of reconciliation. In Luke 4:16–30, Jesus proclaims the messianic kingdom of God. We will first examine 2 Cor 5:16–21 followed by Luke 4:16–30.

This passage, 2 Cor 5:16–21, is best understood in its context within the Pauline epistles. Specifically, this passage hinges on the subject of the frailty of human experience. It is in that context that Paul advances the idea that one day, all of this corruption and weaknesses will be done away with, and newness of life will be experienced not only by humanity, but also by the entire creation. Thus, the new creation discussed in 2 Cor 5:17 will be an answer to the problems related to the old nature of the cosmos as we know it. In this passage, six key terms stand out. The terms are discussed in this section, but not necessarily in the order they are listed here. First is *church*, implied by the word "us" used twice in verse 18. Second is *reconcile*, referring to what Christ did in the past, the effects of which are felt in the present, even though its full realization is in the future. Third is *reconciliation*, that to which the church is called. Fourth is *ambassadors*. Fifth is *ministry*. Last is *righteousness*.

Richard Hays notes that the term "reconciliation" [*katallagēs*], as used by Paul in this passage, is a word drawn from the sphere of politics, which refers to dispute resolution, as in diplomatic reconciliation of warring nations or in personal relationships or the reunion of an estranged husband and wife.[1] As Klyne R. Snodgrass argues, Christ died for all humanity and the ministry of reconciliation is given to all Christians.[2]

Christians share in this ministry of reconciliation, as implied by "us" in 2 Cor 5:14, 18–20, so that they may help to reconcile "all" (2 Cor 5:14, 15) Christ for whom died.

Now that Christians are not only reconciled to God but have also accepted this reconciliation, they are ambassadors of reconciliation. Although the noun form of the word ambassador in Greek is *presbeuteros*, J.D. Douglas notes that *presbeuō* is what is used in 2 Cor 5:20 metaphorically to apply to "the representative of Christ in carrying his message of reconciliation."[3] Having reconciled the world to himself, God now "entrusts the announcement of this reconciliation to those who have come to know it in their lives," giving them both "the ministry and message of reconciliation."[4]

1. Hays, "Word of Reconciliation."
2. Snodgrass, "Reconciliation," 10.
3. Douglas, "Ambassador," 29.
4. Gloer, "Ambassadors of Reconciliation," 598.

Lawrence O. Richards notes that as much as the writer of this epistle was determined to serve as Christ's ambassador in imploring others on Christ's behalf to be reconciled to God, in context, "the appeal for a reconciling ministry is directed to believers."[5] The task of Christian believers is therefore to help the rest of humanity (as well as the entire created order) to be aware of the completed work of reconciliation that God accomplished through Christ's death for all. Thus, Christ's ambassadors "stand in the place of Christ" to proclaim "the call and invitation of God to human beings to be reconciled to God." That is the role of the church and its membership as ambassadors of the kingdom of God.

This is part of the ministry of reconciliation discussed by Paul in 2 Cor 5:16–21. It is also part of the mission of the church as a *kingdom community* in restoring the fallenness of humanity and all creation. Full restoration will only be realized in the future when there will be a full manifestation of the kingdom of God. In the meantime, as we evangelize as ambassadors of reconciliation, we are expected to be involved actively in the partial restoration of the kingdom status. N.T. Wright's view on this issue, with particular reference to Rom 8:17–24, evokes the idea of a *now and not yet* in discourse about the kingdom of God. Wright implies that, in the *now* kingdom, God saves his people so they can be stewards over his present corrupt creation with healing, restorative justice, and love. Ultimately, in the future *not-yet* kingdom, God's good handiwork of creation "will be set free from the slavery that consists in corruption."[6] Wright then goes further to identify three categories of groaning and their respective roles in bringing about reconciliation and the birthing of new creation.

These are the groaning church, a groaning creation, and the groaning Spirit.[7] When these three aspects of groaning are applied to reconciliation, the groaning church is the ambassador of reconciliation while a groaning creation represents the subjects of reconciliation. The groaning Spirit, for his part, empowers the church to do reconciliation. Thus, participation in the kingdom of God implies that, since all creation (humanity included) groans waiting for Christians to manifest who they really are in Christ, it is the duty of Christians to be involved actively in reconciliation, re-orienting the entire creation towards the new creation.

What makes the church a kingdom community? Richard B. Hays refers to the church variously as a "counter-cultural community of discipleship," an embodiment of an "alternative order," and a "primary addressee of God's

5. Richards, *Zondervan Expository Dictionary*, 515.

6. Wright, *Surprised by Scripture*, 88.

7. Wright, *Surprised by Scripture*, 89.

imperatives."[8] Hays adds that since the focus of the biblical story is on God forming a covenant people, the corporate community called church is expected to be a sign of God's redemptive purposes in the world. That way, this community is able to express and experience the presence of the kingdom of God.[9] Larry Rasmussen uses several descriptions of the earliest Christian communities. He sees them as "a new humanity," a new world order, a "third race" beyond Jews and Gentiles that transcends ethnicity and nations, and the "first fruits" of a new age coming to birth in the midst of a dying one.[10] One feature of the church as a kingdom community is its ability to incarnate itself by dwelling in love with its neighbors. This makes "credible witness to the truth of the gospel," which is about love.[11]

As a kingdom community, the church is expected to be an exemplar alternative community that provides an alternative way of living. The idea of an alternative community suggests existence of dysfunctional communities that do not mirror godliness. Therefore, a Christian-shaped community is an alternative way of living that runs contrary to the mainstream communities. This alternative community may be faulty and imperfect. However, this is the model God will use as a witness of what the new creation looks like (1 Cor 5:17). It is this alternative community that God has called to reflect his desire for renewal of all things.

According to Larry Rasmussen, ecclesial practices help to build the church as an alternative community by ministering to people through such things as ordering, caring for, and leading communities for purposes of promoting flourishing of life.[12] This, in itself, is a form of witness for the church as an alternative community. Moreover, some basic functions of the church propel this kingdom community in its mission. These are: witnessing to God's kingdom through proclamation of the gospel of Christ, pointing to God's coming kingdom, being an agent of inception of God's kingdom, and serving as a sign of God's kingdom by modeling the good news in the community of faith.[13]

As God's ambassadors of reconciliation (2 Cor 5:19–20), Christians participate in ministry that embodies and extends the kingdom of God. Richard Stearns observes that God has not only chosen the church to represent him as his ambassadors by proclaiming the "good news," but that

8. Hays, "Scripture-Shaped Community," 47.

9. Hays, "Scripture-Shaped Community," 47.

10. Rasmussen, "Shaping Communities," 127.

11. McKnight, *Kingdom Conspiracy*, 140–141.

12. Rasmussen, "Shaping Communities," 120–121.

13. Sider, *Churches That Make a Difference*, 148–49.

God's people are expected actually to be that "good news," or carriers of the gospel who bring change into the world.[14] We therefore embody the gospel, becoming "the righteousness [*dikaiosýnē*] of God," (2 Cor 5:21). This means that God's people are now liberated "so that they can be God-reflecting, image-bearing, working models of divine covenant faithfulness in action."[15] Thus, our mission as God's people is to represent God as his ambassadors, embodying who he is. In 2 Cor 5:21, God has, through Jesus, "announced that we have his righteousness and works to make us more and more like him."[16]

Since Jesus Christ's resurrection, an event that also offered hope of resurrection to those who believe in him, we can no longer look at him in an earthly way (2 Cor 5:16). Just like there is new hope offered by and in Jesus Christ, there is also newness of life and perspective on the part of those who trust in this Jesus. Hence, this condition reveals the "new creation" (2 Cor 5:17) that God's people bring to bear following the death and resurrection of Jesus Christ. In that sense, followers of Jesus are not only new creation but also God's ambassadors for the new creation intended by God, which leads to the renewal of all things (2 Cor 5:16–21). Richard B. Hays laments how older Bible translations like the King James Version (KJV) and the Revised Standard Version (RSV) mistranslated part of the verse.

Instead of "If anyone is in Christ—New Creation," these versions have: "he is a new creature" (KJV) and "he is a new creation" (RSV). A literal translation ought to treat the words "new creation" as an exclamatory interjection. Otherwise, the intended meaning is distorted, making it appear that Paul's focus here is only to describe the good "personal transformation of the individual through conversion experience."[17] Hays adds that the background of this "new creation" text is Isa 65:17–19, which tells of "Isaiah's fervent prophetic hope for the renewal of the world."[18] Paul's use of "creation" [*ktisis*] refers to the whole created order. This image of "new creation" belongs to the Jewish apocalyptic thought in which "the present age of evil and suffering was to be superseded by a glorious messianic age in which God would prevail over injustice and establish righteousness."[19] In context, the church has entered "the sphere of the eschatological age," making the

14. Stearns, *Hole in Our Gospel*, 3.
15. Wright, *Day the Revolution Began*, 4092.
16. Richards, *Zondervan Expository Dictionary*, 537.
17. Hays, *Moral Vision of the New Testament*, 20.
18. Hays, *Moral Vision of the New Testament*, 20.
19. Hays, *Moral Vision of the New Testament*, 20.

new creation "a present reality."[20] For Paul, this newness is brought about by Christ's cross and resurrection. Henceforth, a re-evaluation of our relationships is called for, and this must be done in light of that transformation.[21]

Regardless of what this "newness" relates to, it is generally agreed that a "convert, as part of a community of faith, enters the cosmic drama of re-creation that God inaugurated at the resurrection of Jesus Christ and will bring to completion at the Parousia."[22] Thus, entrants into this "newness" become active participants in this ongoing recreation drama, thus qualifying them as "ambassadors" of bringing about reconciliation. This is what Paul refers to as the "ministry of reconciliation" that has been entrusted by God to his people. Thus, the ideas of "new creation" and reconciliation are connected in 2 Cor 5:17–19.[23]

The word "ministry" [*diakonia*] in 2 Cor 5:18, as it relates to reconciliation, is worth examining. Lawrence Richards notes that the word ministry has to do with actions of love in service to and on behalf of others.[24] The same God who reconciled us to himself through Christ now gives us that reconciliation so that we can have a ministry of reconciliation as his personal agents of representation in the world.[25] Reconciliation thus experienced is, in a sense, interim, as we await its fullness in the future. Hence the idea of the kingdom as now and not yet. No wonder Christians throughout history have not pretended like they had "arrived" at the ultimate new creation, but rather, with the resurrection of Jesus and the gift of the Spirit, they knew that the anticipated new creation had already broken into the world, a perspective which formed their spirituality and mission.[26] This position is shared by McKnight in his view of "kingdom theology" as it applies to Christian faith. He notes that whereas Christians live "after the inauguration of redemption, so they should be Christike," they also "live in a time when they are not fully outfitted for eternity," and so they still bear the marks of the flesh.[27] That is how the tension in kingdom theology plays out in practice.

Paul discusses new creation and reconciliation within the context of replacement of "the earthly tent" (2 Cor 5:1) with "the "heavenly dwelling" (2 Cor 5:2). Thus, the limitations of this life now, which is earthly [*epigeios*]

20. Hays, *Moral Vision of the New Testament*, 36.

21. Hays, "Word of Reconciliation."

22. Levison, "Creation and New Creation," 190.

23. Richards, *Zondervan Expository Dictionary*, 515.

24. Richards, *Zondervan Expository Dictionary*, 443.

25. McKnight, *Community Called* Atonement, 30.

26. Wright, *Case for the Psalms*, loc. 111.

27. McKnight, *Kingdom Conspiracy*, 42.

or "of the earth" is contrasted with "that which flows from the heavenly realm infused by God and thus is pure in origin and character."[28] It is while in this temporary tent that Christians groan longingly to be "clothed with our heavenly dwelling" (2 Cor 5:2–4). That longing for newness or new creation is in the understanding of what Jesus Christ did for us (2 Cor 5:14–18). The death and resurrection of Jesus signaled the end of the old age and portended the beginning of the new. By implication, "the church is to find its identity and vocation by recognizing its role within the cosmic drama of God's reconciliation of the world to himself."[29] It is this new creation, the church in Christ, that now becomes "the righteousness of God" (2 Cor 5: 21) and which is expressed as a present reality.[30] This perspective, therefore, alters our view of Christ from an earthly perspective, or, as Paul says, a "human point of view" (2 Cor 5:16). Instead, it has to be seen through the new creation lens which is "heavenly" and not "earthly" (2 Cor 5:2–4). It is this new perspective that forms the basis for advancing the gospel of the kingdom, which is the responsibility of the church (2 Cor 5:18–20), and to which all creation is invited to enjoy in being reconciled to its creator.

In summary, 2 Cor 5:16–21 indicates that the task of reconciliation is passed to the church after God reconciled the world to himself through Jesus Christ. The church, therefore, is both the product of this reconciliation as well as its ambassador. Since the church is the means and instrument of that reconciliation, its responsibility is to announce and demonstrate to the created order the act and the result of this reconciliation that God did in Christ long ago. That way, the newness of the creation is demonstrated by those "in Christ," that is, the church. Let us now turn to the second scripture passage, Luke 4:16–30.

The foregoing ministry of reconciliation that Paul points out is what was described in Jesus' own public proclamation of his own ministry in Luke 4:16–30. Luke 4:14–9:51 is the larger pericope from which Luke 4:16–30 is taken. In context, Luke 4:14–9:51 itself demonstrates that Jesus came to fulfill Isaiah's prophecy regarding the Messiah (Luke 4:21). Luke 4:14–44 specifically contextualizes Jesus' ministry "in synagogues" (Luke 4:15, 44). The escape from the mobs (Luke 4:30) opens a door for Jesus to do more ministry of teaching on the Sabbath (Luke 4:31), casting out an unclean spirit (Luke 4:35), healing Peter's mother-in-law (Luke 4:38–39), healing various diseases, and exorcising demons (Luke 4:40–41). All that was done

28. Richards, *Zondervan Expository Dictionary*, 241.

29. Hays, *Moral Vision of the New Testament*, 19.

30. Hays, *Moral Vision of the New Testament*, 36.

as an imperative for Jesus to accomplish his mission of proclaiming good news of the kingdom of God to the poor (Luke 4:43–44).

It is within this context that Luke 4:16–30 is significant. It introduces Jesus' public ministry with a self-annunciation of what his ministry and the mission of the kingdom consist. That announcement was both appalling and surprising to the hearers, triggering a controversy that was to linger on even beyond his earthly life and ministry. Luke 4:16–30 presents Jesus at the beginning of his ministry. Yet, according to Luke 4:14–15, Jesus had already been actively preaching and healing.[31] Luke may have placed the incident recorded in Mark 6:1-6 at the beginning of Jesus' ministry to introduce key themes, such as his rejection by his own people, his suffering, and his mission to the Gentiles.[32]

According to R.T. France, Jesus' appearance in Nazareth may not have been his first public ministry appearance because, most likely, he might have carried on a ministry earlier in Capernaum (as presupposed in Luke 4:23). On the basis of that reputation, he was invited to preach in his home synagogue as a distinguished visitor.[33] At that time, it was customary for a synagogue worship leader to extend invitation to a "worthy person in the congregation to read Scriptures and to comment on the reading," as in the case of Paul and Barnabas in Antioch of Pisidia (Acts 13:15).[34] France further identifies five themes that are at the heart of this passage. These are: (1) Jesus begins his public ministry in Galilee and visits his home village; (2) Jesus declares that he has come to fulfill the vision in Isaiah 61:1–2 of the Lord's anointed; (3) Jesus's ministry is of deliverance and of good news to the poor; (4) the people's initially favorable impression turns to hostility when Jesus insists that his mission is wider than their local concerns; and (5) Jesus survives a murder attempt.[35]

It is in Luke 4:16–30 where Jesus publicly announced who he was and what his mission was about. He intimates that he was the one coming to fulfill the messianic expectation and thereby inaugurate the long-awaited kingdom of God. N.T. Wright refers to this Lukan passage as the "Nazareth Manifesto," based on the Jubilee principle, the focus of which is God rescuing his people from all forms of slavery.[36] The principle was what Moses had announced in the Jubilee codes in Leviticus 25 about God's will regarding

31. Jeffrey, *Luke*, 69.

32. Arnold, *Zondervan Illustrated Bible Backgrounds*, 361.

33. France, *Luke*, 68–69.

34. Bailey, *Jesus through Middle Eastern Eyes*, 147.

35. France, *Luke*, 69.

36. Wright, *How God Became King*, 233.

money and property. Every fifty years, land and property taken must be returned to its original owners for it was inalienably theirs.[37] It is clear from Luke 4:16–30 that Jesus intentionally aligned himself with the prophetic tradition of promoting *shalom* justice, thereby framing "his ministry around the Jubilee year of Leviticus 25," in which, among other things, there was a cancellation of debts and freeing of slaves.[38] Jesus' message of the "year of Jubilee" was the fulfillment of the biblical promise.

It is noteworthy that Jesus' pronouncement took people by surprise, triggering a series of unending controversy and mixed reactions throughout Jesus' earthly ministry. Some people were amazed and spoke "well of him" (Luke 4:22) while others were so "furious" that they "drove him out of the town" and even attempted to kill him by throwing him off the cliff (Luke 4:28–29). Whereas at first the townspeople welcomed their "hometown boy," they later turned against him because they were enraged by his claim that in the past God had sometimes chosen to favor Gentiles over his people, Israel: an allegation that was taken as heretical.[39] This incident marked the beginning of the Great Galilean ministry in Luke 4:14–9:50, during which Jesus "proclaims the message of the kingdom of God, calls disciples and performs miracles demonstrating his kingdom authority."[40]

There have been debates as to whether the passage that Jesus read was pre-selected for him or if he selected it himself. Gail O'Day notes that although by the first century readings from the Torah were already fixed into a lectionary cycle, it is unclear if the prophetic readings, where this passage from Isaiah was taken, were set by this date.[41] It is, therefore, safe to conclude that Jesus intentionally selected his readings so he could purposefully read passages that confirmed who he was and what he had come to accomplish: that he was, indeed, the promised Messiah and that he had come to inaugurate the long-awaited Jewish kingdom. Jesus chose Isa 61:1–2, combined with phrases from Isa 48:8–9, and possibly an allusion to Isa 58:6.[42] Samuel Balentine observes that Jesus not only quoted portions of Isa 61:1–2 and 58:6 texts from the Septuagint, but that he sliced the two together to form one reading and also rearranged their sequence.[43]

37. Florence, *Inscribing the Text*, 27.

38. Salvatierra and Heltzel, *Faith-Rooted Organizing*, 36.

39. Arnold, *Zondervan Illustrated Bible Backgrounds*, 361.

40. Arnold, *Zondervan Illustrated Bible Backgrounds*, 361.

41. O'Day, "Today This Word Is Fulfilled," 358.

42. Jeffrey, *Luke*, 70.

43. Balentine, "He Unrolled the Scroll," 162.

According to O'Day, although Luke presents the words that Jesus read as Scripture, the words that he himself presents are a clear amalgam of texts rather than exact quotations.[44] Whether the passage was pre-selected for Jesus or not, there was divine providence "clearly at work in the chosen text."[45] The phrase "good news to the poor" in verse 18 is a summary of Luke's characteristic emphasis on Jesus' concern for the marginalized.[46] Additionally, as France would further argue, although these Isaianic words of prophecy were read by and fulfilled in Jesus, they could have been understood as references to socio-political liberation as well as spiritual deliverance.[47]

Luke's position is that Jesus came to accomplish as his mission both socio-political as well as spiritual deliverance at a personal level. No wonder the ensuing record of Jesus' actual ministry as reported by Luke focuses on physical and spiritual deliverance of the sick and possessed, on giving hope to the hopeless and a voice to the voiceless rather than on attempting to reform the social or political system.[48] That position notwithstanding, France notes that—although Jesus seemed not to favor that path of dealing with the social-political structural matters, as such—the values expressed therein actually "provided an important incentive to radical Christian socio-political involvement in subsequent generations."[49]

Kevin DeYoung and Greg Gilbert, however, take a somewhat cautious view. They caution Christians against interpreting Jesus' mission as purely social or interpreting it overly literally. In that case, they argue that even though Jesus read in the Scripture that he had come to release the captives, there is no indication anywhere in the Gospels that Jesus actually, literally, set any prisoner free.[50] One would even argue that Jesus did not set free his relative, John the Baptist, who was martyred while in jail.[51] This position, however, does not negate the fact that Jesus was concerned about social aspects of life since his gospel message was a holistic one. The idea behind this view is to caution Bible readers from seeing everything purely through a social lens without paying credence to the spiritual dimension that is central in the biblical narrative.

44. O'Day, "Today This Word Is Fulfilled," 358.

45. Arnold, *Zondervan Illustrated Bible Backgrounds*, 362.

46. France, *Luke*, 71.

47. France, *Luke*, 71.

48. France, *Luke*, 71.

49. France, *Luke*, 71.

50. DeYoung and Gilbert, *What Is the Mission of the Church?*, 39.

51. Wright, *Simply Jesus*, 82; Matt 14:3–10; Mark 6:17–29.

Kenneth Bailey, however, is emphatic that "Jesus' ministry was to break the power of the economic, social, and political chains that kept people in bondage," meaning that the "good news for the poor" he had come to preach about was essentially "release to the captives" and "liberty" for the oppressed.[52] Indeed, a close look at verse 18 shows that Luke chose to use a Greek word transliterated as *ptōchois* and not any other words that would have still meant the poor. According to William J. Barber II, *ptōchois*, meant those made poor by existing systemic policy decisions and by exploitation of those in positions of power.[53] Therefore, Jesus' ministry was not just to get the poor out of poverty but, most importantly, to address the existing socio-political and economic structures that were responsible for subjugating the poor and pushing them to the margins of society.

Jesus' annunciation of his ministry and what he had come to fulfill took the society both by storm and surprise. The words "is now fulfilled" implied fulfillment of that scripture from Isaiah in the perfect tense, describing "an action that is completed in the present moment but that has ongoing significance" because it had been fulfilled "in the present moment of proclamation."[54] Thus, fulfillment of Scripture brought about change. Jesus' message implied socio-political transformation, which is at the very heart of the Christian message.

Socio-political transformation cannot be divorced from the good news the church is called to proclaim. This revolutionary message drove the crowd into anger and violence since they understood well what Jesus was saying. The "present fulfillment" meant that the way they ordered their world would have to change. Gentiles and lepers now had to be accepted as belonging to God's jubilee, which Jesus had announced.[55] The audience rejected Jesus' message. By referring to the stories of Elijah and Elisha in Luke 4:25–27, Jesus noted that God's "favor" was not restricted to Israelites.[56]

Calling for change that reorders one's social, cultural, economic and political perspective is not always well received and, therefore, it is no wonder the hearers reacted the way they did. That explains why, although they may have upheld the sanctity of Scripture read by Jesus, his hearers were not willing to readily accept its demands, especially the immediacy of the fulfillment of this messianic message. Jubilee meant empowering the poor and the marginalized.

52. Bailey, *Jesus through Middle Eastern Eyes*, 157.

53. NC Forward Together Moral Movement Channel, "We Must Raise a Moral Dissent."

54. O'Day, "Today This Word Is Fulfilled," 361.

55. O'Day, "Today This Word Is Fulfilled," 361.

56. Hays, *Moral Vision of the New Testament*, 115.

Jesus' announcement that he was the fulfillment of that Jubilee was more than the hearers could bear since he advocated giving social power, social access, and social goods to the poor and excluded, thereby curbing the hearers' accumulation of material wealth. They did not want to hear about the Jubilee, and were so infuriated that Jesus barely escaped from being thrown off a cliff.[57] From that point onwards, Jesus began a life-long collision course with the societal establishment that was unwilling to change. On the whole, Luke's account of the opening of Jesus' ministry shows it is clearly good news to those living in oppression, whether it is spiritual or political.

Either way, the announcement was good news. It was an announcement of the reign of God and his kingdom, with tangible results on behalf of needy humanity. One unanswered question, however, remains: Does the fact that Jesus did not suggest socio-political reforms mean that we, as his followers, ought not be concerned about oppressive socio-political and economic structural systems? Gregory Boyd argues that most scholars agree that in his announcement of Isaiah's vision of Jubilee, Jesus was referring to the year when all debts would be cancelled, all land lost through indebtedness restored, and all slaves and prisoners set free. Therefore, Jesus was the bringer of this year of Jubilee, unleashing a revolution, which was indeed good news to lower classes.[58]

According to Richard Stearns, what Jesus did in this instance was to declare who he was and what was his mission. That mission included three components: (1) proclamation of the good news of salvation; (2) compassion for the sick and sorrowful; and (3) a commitment to justice. Thus, according to Richard Stearns, God shows his concern for the spiritual, physical, and social dimensions of human beings. This concern is what was squarely Jesus' whole gospel which, by extension, has become the mission of all those who claim to be his followers.[59] In that case, the rule and reign of God as inaugurated by Jesus Christ is evidence of God's commitment to setting his people free, both spiritually and social-politically. Thus, as Scot McKnight has put it, the inauguration of Jesus' ministry in this passage showed that it was through him, the Messiah and King, that God would rule and establish his kingdom, thereby marking "the end of oppressive injustices against the poor, the mourning, and the righteous."[60]

In conclusion, the two passages selected for this study (2 Cor 5:16–21 and Luke 4:18–30) clearly demonstrate that Jesus had inaugurated the long

57. Florence, *Inscribing the Text*, 29.

58. Boyd, *Myth of a Christian Religion*, 107.

59. Stearns, *Hole in Our Gospel*, 21–22.

60. McKnight, *Kingdom Conspiracy*, 192.

awaited kingdom of God and that his disciples, and the church, had been called to be ambassadors to propagate the message of that kingdom. It is noteworthy that throughout the Scriptures, the proclamation of good news of the kingdom is also associated with the miraculous, including healings and, to some extent, freeing people from oppression. That is a vital part of the teaching on reconciliation. In other words, the kingdom of God, which Jesus inaugurated and which the church is expected to advance, shows that God is sovereign and that no other ruler or power or principality is superior to him. Luke 4:16–30 and 2 Cor 5:16–21 both show that the mission of Christ and the theme of reconciliation are together related to the motif of the kingdom of God. The church has the responsibility of advancing the mission of Christ, which, in essence, is reconciliation. This is the heart of the message about the kingdom of God. Jesus Christ had indeed proven that he was not only the expected Messiah or Christ (Luke 4:18; see also Luke 3:22) who had come to save his people, but he now extends the same ministry of reconciliation to his ambassadors: the church.

Followers of Jesus Christ who are freed by God are, therefore, what Noel Castellanos calls champions of justice in this broken world.[61] In this way, the inaugurated kingdom of God is advanced and the ministry of reconciliation is kept alive. And this ministry of the kingdom is what is expected to be continually proclaimed in word and deed by the church, which is now his ambassador charged with bringing about reconciliation.

THEOLOGICAL FOUNDATION

Jesus announced that he was the Messiah who was expected to inaugurate God's kingdom. The kingdom was inaugurated by the coming of Jesus, although its fullness is to be realized in the future new creation. In the meantime, Christians are God's ambassadors of reconciliation, telling this story of how God was in Christ reconciling the world to himself. Thus, since the church has a responsibility in this newly inaugurated kingdom, there is need to explore some pertinent theological concepts in this debate as well as their interrelationship. That is why the concepts of the gospel, the kingdom of God, reconciliation, and the church need to be understood in relation to social justice. More specifically, we need to understand what the kingdom of God is, its relationship with the church, and how it informs our understanding of social justice. The end goal is to help us learn how God's people live out their calling by influencing the society around them for the kingdom of God.

61. Castellanos, *Where the Cross Meets the Street*, loc. 2401.

The word "gospel" [*euangelion*] simply means good news. This term, which Christianity is all about, implies that something has happened as a result of which the world is a different place.[62] This word is mostly used in the Epistles in connection with the saving work of God in Jesus.

When the phrase "of the kingdom" is added to it, the term implies the good news regarding God's kingdom being at hand and the related act of God establishing his rule on earth.[63] Again, and most importantly, the idea of the gospel of the kingdom must focus on the person of Jesus.[64] Thus, the usage of the term gospel must not only be theistic but must additionally be centered on what God does through Jesus Christ. Erickson notes that Pauline theology views the gospel as "centered on Jesus Christ and what God has done through him."[65] This is the good news that the church offers the world: the core vitality defining the church. Moreover, since the gospel is news that brings hope, peace, joy, and satisfaction, the church must preserve it at all costs.[66]

The kingdom of God and the gospel with which it is associated are about reconciliation of the entire created order with God. As the Creator and sustainer of his created order, God invites humans to partner with him in running the cosmos: to renew it and bring about reconciliation. The church is expected to be in the forefront in this partnership of co-operating with God in bringing about this divine vision of renewal of and reconciliation with the cosmos. Christians are, therefore, the appointed ambassadors of this reconciliation effort. They do this this through proclamation of the gospel message.

Erickson challenges us to go beyond the rather narrow definition of the kingdom of God as merely "the reign of God in human hearts wherever obedience to God is found."[67] As George Eldon Ladd would argue, this kingdom is not only about God's reign in the human heart, but it is one that is dynamically active in the person of Jesus and in human history, thus making it present and future, inward and outward, spiritual and apocalyptic.[68] There is therefore tension in understanding what the kingdom is. Ladd reviews various views of what the kingdom of God is and what it is not. He does so by exploring this concept of the kingdom in three distinct yet related

62. Wright, *Simply Good News*, 16.
63. Richards, *Zondervan Expository Dictionary*, 316.
64. Richards, *Zondervan Expository Dictionary*, 379.
65. Erickson, *Christian Theology*, 1072.
66. Erickson, *Christian Theology*, 1075.
67. Erickson, *Christian Theology*, 1163.
68. Ladd, *Presence of the Future*, 42.

categories or phases. These are the prophetic expectation of the kingdom in the Old Testament, the development of this expectation through the intertestamental literature, and a reconstruction of the teaching and mission of Jesus Christ with reference to the kingdom of God.[69]

According to Richards, the usage of the term kingdom [*basileia*] in the New Testament is derived from the Old Testament thought of "a realm in which a king exerts control and authority." By extension, therefore, the kingdom of God portrays the idea of "the realm in which God is in control" rather than as a place.[70] In the New Testament, references to the kingdom of God are always tied to the person and ministry of Jesus Christ.

Ladd notes that the kingdom of God is "primarily the dynamic reign or kingly rule of God" with the church as its community comprising the society of human beings.[71] While not giving a straightforward definition of what the kingdom of God is or is not, Scot McKnight notes that during Jesus' earthly ministry, this long-awaited promise of the kingdom was said to be "already present," yet, at the same time, it was seen as "still in the future."[72] McKnight adds that since this kingdom has already been inaugurated in and through our redemption in Christ, "it can be realized in our world today."[73] Thus, the kingdom of God must be seen both from a present experiential dimension as well as a future perspective.

Howard A. Snyder offers what he considers "six fundamental *tension points* or *polarities*" of the kingdom of God that encompass a wide range of perspectives with a view to being as comprehensive as possible. He summarizes these polarities as follows: (1) present versus future; (2) individual versus social; (3) spirit versus matter; (4) gradual versus climactic; (5) divine action versus human action; and (6) the church's relation to the kingdom.[74] Thus, in Snyder's opinion, the idea of God's reign cuts across a number of dimensions that touch on God's relationship with his creation. By implication, it is therefore not possible to provide a one-dimensional perspective of what the kingdom of God entails since the idea is conceptually multi-dimensional and multi-faceted in nature.

The disciples expected a geo-political messianic kingdom based on the expectation that God would re-establish the kingships of Israel. A geo-political kingdom would involve land, people, nation, law, temple, leadership,

69. Ladd, *Presence of the Future*, 42.

70. Richards, *Zondervan Expository Dictionary*, 378.

71. Ladd, *Presence of the Future*, 262.

72. McKnight, *Kingdom Conspiracy*, 10.

73. McKnight, *Kingdom Conspiracy*, 11.

74. Snyder, *Models of the Kingdom*, 1617.

and strategy.[75] The disciples were incorrect because, as Wyndy Corbin Reuschling notes, the kind of kingdom Jesus had in mind "would not be defined by or restricted to the politics of nation-states," but rather "would be based on the power and work of the Holy Spirit."[76] That view also explains why "the kingdom and Jesus are inseparable" in that it does not make sense to talk about a kingdom without a king.[77]

In order to understand what is the nature of the kingdom of God, Snyder further offers eight models for resolving those apparent dialectical tensions. He thus sees the kingdom as: (1) future hope; (2) inner spiritual experience; (3) mystical communion; (4) institutional church; (5) countersystem; (6) political state; (7) Christianized culture; and (8) earthly utopia.[78] Thus, Snyder helps to simplify the understanding of the kingdom of God in the church so that the rule of God can be practical and not abstract. This is especially so in the case of ordinary Christians who are keen on experiencing the presence and the workings of God in their lives here and now. There is need, therefore, to understand what the church is and how it relates to the idea of the kingdom of God.

From a historical, biblical, and theological perspective, the Greek term translated "church" [*ekklesia*] was not initially and etymologically a Christian word. In Greek, the word simply denoted "a public assembly summoned by a herald," while in the Hebrew usage it brought the idea of a congregation or a gathering of people of Israel.[79] With time, however, the term came to imply that body associated with followers of Jesus Christ, especially as used in Pauline epistles and in later references to the growing body of Christian believers.

The concepts of church and the kingdom of God are related and, therefore, tend to be confused. This relationship gets even more complicated when the idea of gospel is added. Thus, the themes of church, kingdom (of God), and gospel often overlap as a careful study of the New Testament and church history would reveal. For example, it is common to talk of the church as having the responsibility of preaching the gospel of the kingdom of God. Usage of these concepts is also taken for granted, especially within ecclesial circles.

One reason why the concept of church and its mission is not well understood is because of a lack of a clear distinction between the church

75. Reuschling, "Christian Ethical Commitments."

76. Reuschling, "Christian Ethical Commitments," 214.

77. Richards, *Zondervan Expository Dictionary*, 379.

78. Snyder, *Models of the Kingdom*, 18.

79. Bromiley, *International Standard Bible Encyclopedia*, 693.

and the kingdom of God, especially due to the Roman Catholic Church's traditional view of the two as being synonymous.[80] D. Martyn Lloyd-Jones maintains, however, that the church is an expression of the kingdom since the kingdom is much broader than church.[81] Daniel J. Harrington, on his part, puts this distinction very well:

> While the Church does not replace the kingdom of God, its origin and mission are intimately tied with the kingdom of God. The Church is the community of those gathered in the name of Jesus Christ. It arose from Jesus' proclamation of God's kingdom and has as its mission sharing Jesus' vision of God's kingdom with others. The Church may be described as those who aspire to God's kingdom and are gathered in the name of Jesus and led by the power of the Spirit. . . The Church is not the same as the kingdom of God. Nor does it replace God's kingdom. But without the kingdom of God as proclaimed by Jesus, the Church has no identity or reason for existence.[82]

Similarly, Jürgen Moltmann's perspective is that, in the long-run, church is "a way and a transition to the kingdom of God," thus providing an experiential and a practical life in "eschatological anticipation of the kingdom."[83] Thus, the mission of the church is derived from the mission of God.

Although humanity's Fall severed the cordial relationship between humanity and the Creator, God instituted a mechanism for restoring that relationship, beginning with Israel. The intent here was to form a special people so as to bring total reconciliation of humans to himself, to one another, and to the rest of creation.

This ongoing reconciliation will be fully realized in the future when God's people and the entire creation will be reconciled to their Creator; that is, when the time of new creation coming to fruition, the fullness of God's salvation will be realized. Meanwhile, as the church promotes the kingdom of God, individual believers are also continually transformed into effective ambassadors and faithful citizens of that kingdom. That is why Christopher D. Marshall extrapolates this idea by referring to the whole of humankind as "God's royal vice-regent in the world."[84] The gospel of the kingdom of God is about promoting God's reign, which is the church's mission.

80. Lloyd-Jones, *Church and the Last Things*, 3.
81. Lloyd-Jones, *Church and the Last Things*, 4.
82. Harrington, *Church according to the New Testament*, 20.
83. Moltmann, *Church in the Power of the Spirit*, 35.
84. Marshall, *Crowned with Glory and Honor*, 58.

Cheryl M. Peterson reminds us that the church is not a human creation but, rather, originates from God who then uses human beings to create it and serve God's mission, or *missio Dei*.[85] According to John Driver, the church is a community of humanity that experiences and communicates God's saving intentions.[86] Furthermore, the Scriptures identify various "complementary images of the people of God," which is a reminder that the church has one mandate: to help bring change as a community of transformation.[87] Thus, the world can experience change through the activities of God's people both in word and deed.

Ladd elucidates the idea of the relationship between the kingdom and the church by identifying five distinctive markers.[88] First, he notes that the church is not the kingdom. As the present sphere of God's rule, the kingdom is invisible whereas the church is empirical.[89] Second, the kingdom creates the church. Drawing from the parables of "draw net" and "tares" (from Matthew 13), Ladd notes that although the empirical church comprises "the people of the Kingdom," some of them are not ideal "sons of the Kingdom."[90] Third, the church witnesses to the kingdom. As its mission, the church witnesses to "God's redeeming acts in Christ both past and future."[91] Fourth, the church is the instrument of the kingdom. After Easter and Pentecost, the blessings and powers of the kingdom, as well as the presence of Christ, were "now available to all believers, regardless of the limitations of time and space."[92] Fifth, the church is the custodian of the kingdom. Those who accept the kingdom become the true sons of the kingdom and thereby enter into the enjoyment of its powers and blessings.[93] Additionally, the church acts as the gatekeeper to the kingdom. It has been granted the means of allowing entry or exclusion of others to enter and participate in the realm of the blessings of the kingdom.[94] The church-kingdom relationship is such that the two entities are related and neither exists without the other. The rule of God and the fellowship of humans who have acknowledged this rule are distinct yet interrelated.[95]

85. Peterson, *Who Is the Church?*, 37.
86. Driver, *Images of the Church in Mission*, 12.
87. Driver, *Images of the Church in Mission*, 16.
88. Ladd, *Presence of the Future*, 263–77.
89. Ladd, *Presence of the Future*, 264.
90. Ladd, *Presence of the Future*, 265.
91. Ladd, *Presence of the Future*, 266.
92. Ladd, *Presence of the Future*, 272.
93. Ladd, *Presence of the Future*, 274.
94. Ladd, *Presence of the Future*, 275.
95. Ladd, *Presence of the Future*, 277.

While acknowledging that the church and the kingdom are not one and the same thing, McKnight maintains that kingdom work cannot be accomplished outside the church, since there can be no kingdom outside the church. For him, kingdom mission is first and foremost church mission.[96] McKnight also notes that debates abound about two approaches associated with the kingdom of God: on social justice and related activism on the one hand and about the redemptive moments under Christ on the other.[97] In that case, McKnight challenges what he calls the "Skinny Jeans prevailing and seemingly uncorrectable" definition of the kingdom, narrowly perceived as merely good deeds done by good people (Christian or not) in the public sector for the common good whose focus is on "working for social justice and peace."[98] Hence, the kingdom of God and acts associated with it are necessarily centered both on the church and on God's people, that is, the church. Similarly, Amy L. Sherman offers a sharp critique of what she refers to as a "too-narrow gospel" in evangelicalism that tends to limit the gospel of the kingdom to personal justification. She argues that the gospel of the kingdom, which defined Jesus's work, was not exclusively about individual salvation but about the wider "cosmic redemption and renewal of all things," including our reconciliation with a holy God, with one another and with creation itself.[99] Timothy Keller echoes this view by noting that this world is not simply a theater for individual conversion narratives. Rather, God loves and cares for this material world so much that "the ultimate purpose of Jesus is not only individual salvation and pardon for sins but also the renewal of this world, the end of disease, poverty, injustice, violence, suffering, and death."[100]

N.T. Wright is correct in observing that the gospel of Jesus Christ (as it relates to the kingdom of God) comes as news within a larger context. The kingdom of God points to a wonderful new future while introducing a new period of waiting that changes our expectations.[101] This period of waiting is the realm of the present kingdom of God, prior to its fullness that comes in the future, that is, the not-yet kingdom. Meanwhile, it is this new message the church is called to convey and embody as disciples of Jesus Christ who go about their lives as ambassadors of the gospel in word and deed.

96. McKnight, *Kingdom Conspiracy*, 95.
97. McKnight, *Kingdom Conspiracy*, 18.
98. McKnight, *Kingdom Conspiracy*, 4.
99. Sherman, *Kingdom Calling*, 67.
100. Keller, *Prodigal God*, 190.
101. Wright, *Simply Good News*, 4.

The idea of the church as having a definite God-ordained role in society as far as the kingdom of God is concerned is articulated well by Gregory Boyd. He argues that while Jesus was on earth he was the very embodiment of the kingdom, but when he ascended into heaven he "acquired a collective body" called the church to be "his hands, mouth, and feet operating in the world today."[102] So, the kingdom of God continues to manifest the life of Christ today, but this time through his corporate body, the church.

N.T. Wright is very candid that the primary reason for the existence of the church is two-fold: to worship God and to work for God's kingdom in the world. He adds, however, that the church also exists for another purpose: fellowship among believers. Fellowship, Wright argues, helps in worshipping God and in working for his kingdom in a number of ways. These include encouraging and building one another in faith; praying with and for one another; and learning from and teaching one another. Fellowship would also include setting one another examples to follow, challenges to take up, and urgent tasks to perform.[103] All these tasks contribute to the church's worship of God and involvement in God's kingdom work.

Any candid discussion of the kingdom of God cannot be presented honestly without a clear appreciation of the completed work of reconciliation that God did through Jesus Christ, and which he now continues to accomplish through his church under the enabling power of the Holy Spirit. Avery Dulles unequivocally notes that the kingdom of God is not a human product but, rather, one that is inseparable from Christ and the church.[104] The latter has been described as "the seed, sign, and instrument of the kingdom."[105] The church is, therefore, God's agency in bringing the manifestation of this kingdom on the earth. That means that the centrality of Jesus Christ and what he did, and continues to do through the church, regarding kingdom work cannot be overemphasized. McKnight critiques approaches to kingdom work that remove the role of Jesus Christ and the church in the creation of God's kingdom. McKnight recognizes the nature of the kingdom of God and Jesus Christ's centrality in the establishment of that kingdom:

> Anyone who calls what they are doing "kingdom work" but who does not present Jesus to others or summon others to surrender themselves to King Jesus as Lord and Savior is simply not doing kingdom mission or kingdom work. They are probably doing

102. Boyd, *Myth of a Christian Religion*, 17.
103. Wright, *Simply Christian*, 210.
104. Dulles, *Models of the Church*, 239.
105. Dulles, *Models of the Church*, 239.

> good work and doing social justice, but until Jesus is made known, it is not kingdom mission.[106]

Healing and restoration of what has been broken by sin is God's ongoing project of the work of justice, of restoring and reconciling creation, thereby bringing about the kingdom of God as originally envisioned by the Creator. Bringing order, and therefore God's *shalom*, righteousness, and justice, in an otherwise disorderly creation following the Fall is the goal of God's mission. And this is the mission he has extended to the church, which is his agent for this vital task. This explains why God was himself in Christ not only reconciling the world to himself, but that he also entrusted to his people that "ministry of reconciliation" (2 Cor 5:18–20).

In this regard, one thing that needs to be noted is that the kingdom of God is not brought about through human effort, but rather through God's intervention so that the best that God's people, the church, can do in this "kingdom business" is to co-operate and be in partnership with God's ongoing project. Indeed, God's kingdom work is God's work accomplished in God's own good time.[107] Thus, human beings are not "mere spectators on God's work in the world"; rather, their "deeds of justice will act as concrete demonstrations of what God is going to do, and in fact is already doing now, partly through these deeds themselves."[108] This empowers the church to do kingdom work. And this is exactly what J. Jireh Ministries Church of Columbus, Ohio, is doing.

In conclusion, it is important to note that an appreciation of the concept of the kingdom of God must begin with an understanding of who God is, what his mission is, and, by extension, what the mission of his people is. In a sense, the kingdom of God has three dimensions: (1) past dimension, demonstrating God's continuous reign, even when people neither acknowledged him nor realize that he was at work; (2) present dimension, where God continues to be active in God's people (see Luke 10:9); and (3) eschatological dimension, when God's full sovereignty will be experienced in the future.

Therefore, when we talk about the kingdom of God, it is about humans allowing God to rule and reign both in their personal lives and in society as a whole. This might not always be apparent in society because humans have not acknowledged God's sovereignty. The church, therefore, as part of humanity and God's representative in society, has a great responsibility for helping to initiate the kingdom of God. Failure to partner with God will

106. McKnight, *Kingdom Conspiracy*, 142.

107. Marshall, *Crowned with Glory and Honor*, 115.

108. Marshall, *Crowned with Glory and Honor*, 115.

mean that God's kingdom is not evident in society. The concept of the kingdom is, therefore, the human way of explaining God's sovereignty and reign over creation. The kingdom of God is about God's *shalom* and his salvation, and that is what the gospel of the kingdom seeks to proclaim.

This proclamation is the central mission of the church, the agency charged with the responsibility of representing and advancing the kingdom of God. It is about the church representing the kingdom of God and his *shalom* and salvation. Adeney-Riskotta provides some examples of some of the kingdom undertakings that the church is expected to carry out, among these being opposition to sexism, poverty, human rights abuses, and racism.[109] We in the twenty-first century cannot afford to deviate from this *missio Dei,* which, by extension, is the mission of God's people.

HISTORICAL FOUNDATION

One cannot discuss the concept of the kingdom of God without a candid discussion of righteousness and justice. It is when righteousness and justice are promoted by the church that the kingdom of God is manifested in society. God's reign and rule become evident in practical ways through the lives of God's people. Throughout history, the church has come to appreciate the need for promotion of these two concepts as a way of advancing the claims of the kingdom of God. There are ample historical examples that illustrate and embody the connections between justice and the church's kingdom mission. As Diana Butler Bass notes, the close relationship between personal salvation and political justice became clearer in the sixteenth century so that there was no way a person could be reconciled with God without the society around them being equally affected.[110] Bass is quick to note that this emphasis on social justice lingered on, and actually "remained a theological cornerstone of Protestant practice" for years to come.[111] In other words, personal salvation and social justice were two sides of the same coin.

The church has historically met the needs of people because of its understanding of the mission and ministry of justice and reconciliation. For example, Robertson McQuilkin notes that for the first three centuries of Christianity, the church was actively involved in taking care of the needs of the very people who were persecuting it. Early Christians were active in such practices of ministry as almsgiving, support of widows, caring for the sick and disabled, care for prisoners and slaves, providing work for the

109. Adeney-Riskotta, *Strange Virtues*, 187.

110. Bass, *People's History of Christianity*, loc. 2450.

111. Bass, *People's History of Christianity*, loc. 2498.

unemployed, caring for those who were suffering from calamities, and providing hospitality to those on journeys.[112]

Diana Butler Bass also notes that throughout the first five centuries of its existence, the Christian church was understood primarily as "a way of life in the present," with Christians being referred to as "the People of the Way" because they practiced their faith to such an extent that Christianity actually "changed and improved the lives of adherents."[113] Such actions were a faithful witness of the role of the church in society, challenging even non-believers. Even the pagan emperor Julian had this to say about the church's practices of hospitality: "[t]hese godless Galileans feed not only their own poor but ours."[114] What a powerful testimony of the role the church played then, and still plays today, in being the salt of the earth and the light of the world.

Victor V. Claar and Robin J. Klay note that although democracy and free markets are among humanity's greatest social inventions, they are not sufficient for societies to thrive. Rather, the well-being of society also depends on the presence of dynamic moral and cultural institutions that "produce social glue that unites and equips people for common action based on shared social values."[115] And this is how the church has played its rightful role in society throughout history, by providing this moral link that is missing from the public and private sectors. J. Jireh Ministries Church of Columbus, Ohio, is an example of how the church fills this void.

Over the years, the church has been actively involved in initiating the kingdom of God by presenting the gospel holistically through an integration of social and spiritual aspects. Nevertheless, there have been controversies regarding the extent to which the church should be involved in social issues. Questions have been raised over whether the church should keep out of "the messy business" of social issues, which has resulted in "periodic pendulum swings between withdrawal from the world and outright culture warfare."[116]

Justice and Advocacy in the Church

The predominantly African-American community that lives in the area where JJMC is located is bedeviled by a combination of diverse social, economic, political, and economic challenges. In that regard, an honest

112. McQuilkin, *Introduction to Biblical Ethics*, 448.
113. Bass, *People's History of Christianity*, loc. 461.
114. McQuilkin, *Introduction to Biblical Ethics*, 448.
115. Claar and Klay, *Economics in Christian Perspective*, 214.
116. Wagenman, "Abraham Kuyper," loc. 811.

understanding of the issues involved and approaches to devising strategies for dealing with those challenges requires one to look through the historical lens of the African-American struggle with systemic injustices that have afflicted this community. That means that even an apparently simple matter as dealing with unemployment or security concerns must be understood within the context of the broader subject of civil liberties and racial justice that have played a central role in placing residents of the community of Kimball Farms where they are today. This is a reality that one cannot escape from if the poverty and helplessness that currently exists in this neighborhood are to be addressed so as to enable local residents to not only know about the kingdom of God, but to also experience it in real and practical ways.

Promotion of social justice and human rights has a long history in America. Without a doubt, Christian convictions have played a central role in inculcating this sense of active engagement in civil matters and thus infusing related values and responsibilities that go with them to the wider society. For instance, it was during the Great Awakening that Protestant Christians, mostly those of Anabaptist and Quaker traditions, declined to be involved in the war because of their conviction that any form of violence was unacceptable.[117] Anti-slavery movements and abolitionism as part of upholding human dignity were also catching momentum among churches.[118] No doubt, influential Christian persons advanced this cause for social justice and civil liberties. Notable among these was the contribution of the Christian evangelist, Charles Finney (1792–1875).

Finney's resistance to slavery alongside the Oberlin abolitionists made significant contributions towards shaping the future of the social movement dedicated to upholding human rights and emancipation.[119] Oberlin College in Ohio is particularly singled out as an abolitionist institution and "the first integrated college in the nation."[120] Finney's strong anti-slavery feelings were particularly expressed at Oberlin College, where he served as president and, hence, attracted many disciples to abolitionism.[121] Keith J. Hardman notes that one of Finney's major contributions to the anti-slavery movement was "his provision of an ideological or theological framework upon which abolitionist ideas could be made to interface with Christian doctrine."[122]

117. McGrath, *Protestant Revolution*, 161.
118. McGrath, *Protestant Revolution*, 324.
119. Shelley, *Church History in Plain Language*, 389.
120. Horton and Horton, *Slavery*, 163.
121. Shelley, *Church History in Plain Language*, 389.
122. Hardman, *Charles Grandison Finney*, 369.

Finney's evangelistic campaigns had a major impact upon Protestant social consciousness. Unfortunately, his ardent support of the abolitionist cause was not widely embraced by some churches, which were still jittery about the then-thorny issue of slavery.[123] This did not dampen his enthusiasm for preaching against slavery, a social evil that degraded human beings. On the whole, however, there was a general commitment by the church to address civil rights and social justice.

In the city of Columbus, Ohio, the expanding urban population meant that there was a growing need for addressing pertinent issues on the welfare of the local population. This was particularly so in the case of urban workers who were taking advantage of increased opportunities for employment in the expanding industrial and commercial sectors.[124] The church was inspired by a sense of Christian responsibility to address the ensuing human needs in the city.

Thus, there existed early signs of the church's commitment to justice and civil rights in the public arena as its contribution towards the common good. Of special interest was the initiatives of Washington Gladden (1836–1918), a religious leader who came to Columbus, Ohio, to serve the First Congregational Church at Broad and Fourth Streets. Gladden was deeply committed to social justice and social change.[125] The activist approach of Gladden and other like-minded church leaders came to be referred to as "social gospel," with the city of Columbus being at the center of this movement.[126] During Washington Gladden's 1882–1914 tenure as Pastor of First Congregational Church, Columbus's most successful businessmen heard him preach the social gospel, with its critique of capitalism. During this time, he also served a term on the city council.[127]

Dealing with "labor struggle firsthand" and industrial strife in Columbus, Gladden's evening addresses focused on this labor-relations problem. He did so on the conviction that "the teachings of Jesus contained the principles for the right ordering of society."[128] Bruce L. Shelley defends Gladden by noting that he was not a socialist since he supported private property and private enterprise. However, he was also convinced that there was need for many industries to be run co-operatively while "railroads, mines, and public

123. Bohi, "A Lentz," 546–47.

124. Lentz, *Columbus*, 100.

125. Lentz, *Columbus*, 102.

126. Lentz, *Columbus*, 103.

127. Klein, *Be It Remembered*, 126.

128. Shelley, *Church History in Plain Language*, 413.

service industries of the cities should be operated by the government."[129] One critique of Gladden's theology of social justice was his conviction that, in an effort to apply Christ's principles to the social order, it was perfectly in order to use, "if necessary, the force of the state to intervene for the well-being of society."[130]

Shelley notes that the emerging social justice movement, of which the social gospel was part, was popular among liberal Protestant pastors and theological professors. In that sense, Shelley adds that since the social gospel is "the belief that God's saving work included corporate structures as well as personal lives," Christians have a religious responsibility and obligation "to work for the reconstruction of the social order."[131] As a church leader, Gladden performed his duty of helping his congregation and all those who heard by preaching on the need to have an ordered society that was centered on biblical social justice.

Another church leader who had shaped the social justice landscape among African-Americans in the United States was Reverday C. Ransom (1861–1959). This prominent African-American leader of the African Methodist Episcopal (AME) Church was very instrumental in promoting the cause of justice among Americans of color, especially black Americans. Ransom is specifically ranked among prominent black church advocates of the social gospel movement, whose premise was that "Christianity has a social mission to transform the social structures of society in the direction of equality, freedom, and community."[132]

Ransom's early interest in social justice almost landed him in trouble when he was a student at Oberlin College. In 1882, soon after transferring from Wilberforce College to Oberlin College, Ransom's involvement in student activism rubbed the college authorities the wrong way, resulting in his expulsion. His crime was "organizing and addressing a protest meeting" over segregated eating facilities.[133] He returned to Wilberforce where he continued with his studies and eventually graduated in 1886.[134] In his postgraduation Christian service experience, Ransom continued to apply his social justice skills by serving in various pastorates and in a variety of leadership positions he held over the span of his life. Indeed, David Wills notes that by the time of Ransom's retirement from active ministry in 1952, he was

129. Shelley, *Church History in Plain Language*, 413.

130. Cairns, *Christianity through the Centuries*, 425.

131. Shelley, *Church History in Plain Language*, 413.

132. Dorrien, *Social Ethics in the Making*, 60.

133. Wills, "Reverdy C. Ransom," 188.

134. Wills, "Reverdy C. Ransom," 189.

satisfied that the AME church he had served was now "far better prepared for the struggles of the 1960s," although this church may not have been "the militant and activistic community he would have wished it to be."[135]

The allusion here is to the civil rights struggles that would ensue shortly. It has been rightly remarked that Ransom's pioneering work with the social gospel has enabled black churches to find "a map for making inroads in the modern scope of human need and potential."[136] It is no wonder that, with time, this trend gained momentum, as seen in the American civil rights activities of the 1950s and 1960s when Martin Luther King Jr., among other civil rights workers, fought racial injustice by deliberately opposing and violating segregation laws. Their activism had a ripple effect that led to remarkable achievement in promoting civil rights.[137]

Martin Luther King Jr. (1929–1968) is another example of faith-inspired leaders who were "motivated by the way of Jesus" and whose social justice initiatives helped to develop a structure for the activities of the Civil Rights Movement and faith-based organizing.[138] King had arrived in Montgomery in 1954 to take up a pastorate after studying for his doctorate at Boston University.[139] His involvement in civil rights was unintentional. As much as he had studied about social justice in Boston, his involvement in social activism was triggered by the action of Rosa Parks, an African-American who is today regarded as a true icon of the Civil Rights Movement in America.

On December 1, 1955, long after King's arrival in Montgomery as a Baptist minister, Parks refused to yield her seat on a bus to a white passenger. Parks was evidently tired after a hard day's work.[140] However, according to Palmer J. Parker, Parks' action resulted from a tiredness of soul, a tiredness of consenting to being treated as a lesser being. In refusing to give up her seat, she acted in solidarity with, and in the context of, her oppressed community. It was an act of shared concern as well as a theory of non-violent social change.[141]

Parks' action triggered a chain of events that had far-reaching ripple effects on the cause of social justice. The name of Martin Luther King Jr. was

135. Wills, "Reverdy C. Ransom," 205.

136. Pinn, *Making the Gospel Plain*, 5.

137. De Santis, "Civil Rights," 906–10; Noll, *God and Race in American Politics*, 138–41.

138. Salvatierra and Heltzel, *Faith-Rooted Organizing*, 11.

139. Brock and Young, *Pacifism in the Twentieth Century*, 233.

140. Brock and Young, *Pacifism in the Twentieth Century*, 233.

141. Palmer, *Healing the Heart of Democracy*, 185.

thrown into the limelight as a crusader for social justice due to his leadership role in the ensuing bus boycott. The arrest, trial, and jailing of Parks triggered a great indignation among Montgomery's 50,000 blacks "who had long been subjected to similar treatment of an arbitrary nature."[142]

Subsequently, black leaders, among them Martin Luther King, called for a one-day bus boycott. The boycott's "almost a hundred percent" success encouraged an indefinite extension of this non-violent "act of passive resistance, but not one of civil disobedience, for no law was broken."[143] With King at the helm of this non-violent resistance campaign against racial injustice, the Montgomery mass movement started a chain reaction with similar non-violent assertions of civil rights by the black communities of other Southern cities. As a result, several cities began to take steps to actually desegregate their bus systems.[144] This was a huge success on the part of King and other civil rights leaders in their campaigns for justice and equality.

Besides being impacted by Jesus' teaching on non-violence, especially the Sermon on the Mount on loving one's enemies, King was greatly influenced by three individuals. Two were pacifist professors at Boston University, Dean Walter Muelder and Allen Knight Chalmers. The third person who influenced him was Mahatma Gandhi and his non-violent resistance campaigns.[145] King's Christian commitment as tempered by the social gospel movement influenced him to see "Christianity as a force that could transform not only the individual but the whole of society."[146]

The path toward the promotion of social justice and civil rights was not easy for King. While King was fighting for the realization of constitutionally guaranteed rights, he became frustrated by the web of legal and political obstacles that hindered full emancipation. Those stumbling blocks needed to be overcome before there could be full realization of freedoms, especially for the blacks. He was especially frustrated by a lack of support by some church leaders who, apparently, were not following the same path of emancipation he was pursuing. Thus, King was very disappointed when he wrote the now-famous April 16, 1963 "Letter from Birmingham City Jail" because of apparent disunity among white Christians, especially the leadership, concerning the quest for civil liberties and racial justice.[147]

142. Brock and Young, *Pacifism in the Twentieth Century*, 232.

143. Brock and Young, *Pacifism in the Twentieth Century*, 232.

144. Brock and Young, *Pacifism in the Twentieth Century*, 235.

145. Brock and Young, *Pacifism in the Twentieth Century*, 233.

146. Roberts, "Martin Luther King," 606.

147. Washington, *Testament of Hope*, 298–99.

Moreover, he decried the apparent disinterest by his fellow clergy who, by their opposition to the demonstrations taking place in Birmingham, were, therefore, chided for being content with the superficial kind of social analysis that deals merely with effects without grappling with underlying causes.[148] He therefore called for those church leaders to be in the forefront to advocate for justice since, as he noted, "[i]njustice anywhere is a threat to justice everywhere."[149]

There is need to acknowledge the significant gains that accrued directly and indirectly from this activism that King was a part of. For example, the passing of the Civil Rights Act of 1964 and the Voting Rights Act of 1965 actually "destroyed the legal framework of racial inequality in the United States," thus giving blacks significant power they had not had before.[150] The Civil Rights Act of 1964, in particular, guaranteed racial equality as well as equal opportunity in employment and education. This marked a significant breakthrough for the Civil Rights Movement that King and other fellow black church ministers were a part of.

As Robert H. Mayer notes, this piece of legislation offered optimism for African-Americans because it seemed to promise "a richer involvement in areas of life long denied to black Americans" in two key areas: ending segregation of public facilities and opening up new employment opportunities for African-Americans and women.[151] The benefits of this legislation may have been slow in coming. Thankfully, even though there are some vestiges of past racial oppression, there is much for which to be grateful. It is remarkable that it was that same year of the passing of the Civil Rights Act that King received the Nobel Peace Prize. This was in recognition of King's commitment to fighting for justice through non-violent means as implied in the Award Ceremony Speech given by the Chairman of the Nobel Committee.[152]

The example of King's involvement in social justice is a lesson to Christian leaders on how to shape and influence communities and society in general for the common good. This is particularly so when we consider that his participation in civil rights was an unintended consequence of the social demands of the day.[153] King was not only at peace with God but he also extended this peace to others, especially his enemies, in order to

148. Washington, *Testament of Hope*, 290.

149. Washington, *Testament of Hope*, 290.

150. Brock and Young, *Pacifism in the Twentieth Century*, 240.

151. Mayer, *Civil Rights Act*, 16.

152. Jahn, "Award Ceremony Speech."

153. Mayer, *Civil Rights Act*, 15.

promote reconciliation and build stronger communities. He had a vision of the beloved community.[154] King spent the rest of his life organizing, leading, and rallying grassroots support for civil liberties. One wonders how events would have turned out without the input of this key figure, or if the Civil Rights Movement would have proceeded without him. Long after his death, King's "vision of redemption, reconciliation, and the creation of beloved community" continues to live on.[155]

History has much to teach us regarding the struggles of God's people for spiritual, social, and economic emancipation to open doors for flourishing of humanity. On the whole, there is every reason to be grateful for the church's contributions to the promotion of social justice, especially among African-Americans who have had a long history of waging a protracted war against systemic racial injustices. In retrospect, involvement of the church in the Civil Rights Movement and advocacy was in a sense an attempt to bring a Christian consciousness in the society through building a theistic perspective of the issues at stake at that time.

CONCLUSION

The church has realized the need to ensure that the gospel is relevant and that it addresses challenges that believers face in their everyday lives. In that regard, discussion on the kingdom of God can sometimes fail to capture the essence of the need to have the experiential part in the here and now without necessarily focusing on the future. This explains why H. Richard Niebuhr is at pains to explain that Jesus' most radical statements in Scripture were not closely connected with expectancy of the coming kingdom, as such, but rather on the realization of "the present rule of God in the course of daily and natural events."[156]

Unless the kingdom of God is seen to have an application and relevance to everyday life and struggles that God's people go through in this life, then the gospel is not good news. All it can promise is a good life in the yonder. Christians of all shades need to have one fundamental conviction about the nearness of the kingdom of God rather than to its relative ineffectiveness in power and its remoteness in time or space.[157] The kingdom of God is not only near but it is also present, as much as its fullness may not be comprehended at the moment. This understanding is what gives the

154. King, *Strength to Love*, 115–16.

155. Marsh, *Welcoming Justice*, 27–28.

156. Niebuhr, *Christ and Culture*, 22.

157. Niebuhr, *Christ and Culture*, 65.

gospel of the kingdom of God an enduring timeless freshness and relevance to every generation.

From the foregoing discussion, promoting social justice as part of the mission of the church is what makes the kingdom of God not only something to understand but also to experience. The church would do well to play its rightful role in ensuring that this is done. There are ample biblical foundations for doing that and certainly plenty of theological underpinnings that attest to the need for a seamless integration of social justice and the kingdom of God as part of the mission of the church. Moreover, throughout history, the church has been involved in acts of social justice and reconciliation as a manifestation of the presence and workings of the kingdom of God.

Chapter 3 will pick up these themes. It will look at the contemporary aspects of promoting the kingdom of God using social justice as its vehicle. Emphasis is placed on the American church, particularly within the urban context.

Chapter 3

Review of the Literature

SINCE THE PURPOSE OF this project was to discover how J. Jireh Ministries Church of Columbus, Ohio, influences the local community for the kingdom of God, it is necessary to find out what contemporary literature says with regard to this subject. What is the church doing to fulfill her mission to impact and influence the society for the kingdom of God? To what extent is the church a true and effective agent of God in bringing the ethos of the kingdom of God into society? These are the issues that this section on contemporary literature examines. The aim is to find out how JJMC, the church in general, and other church groups, organizations, and congregations are fulfilling the mission of the church.

God's people are doing much to live up to their mission as ambassadors of reconciliation. It is encouraging to note that the church of today has retained an effective witness in society. It is continuing to be a faithful prophetic voice by living out the gospel of the kingdom in word and deed. In order to appreciate what the church of the twenty-first century is doing to carry out her mission, it is important to understand the relationship between the church, the kingdom of God, and social justice. Of particular interest in this study is examining two issues. First is how social justice is connected and disconnected from the church. Second is seeking to understand how one can be spiritual or religious but indifferent to social justice. Interestingly, Nicholas Wolterstorff notes that the Bible neither defines justice nor provides a theory of justice. It merely assumes that lovers of Scripture know well enough the meaning of this concept.[1]

Therefore, when Christians fail to practice justice, it is an indicator of either a lack of understanding of the Scriptures or, possibly, an intentional abdication of one's responsibility and mission as a follower of Jesus Christ. Being involved in social justice is not a calling for a select group. It is expected of all who are disciples of Jesus because this is the natural thing to do. But one wonders why this is not as obvious. Why are acts of social justice not practiced openly, as one would expect? A good example is evangelicalism with its two fundamental emphases.

The first is its emphasis on experiencing personal conversion through belief in Christ and his work on the cross. The second is a commitment to the authority of Scripture as the infallible guide for Christian faith and practice.[2] Ironically, in real life situations, evangelicalism exhibits a profound mismatch between belief and practice. Apparently, the evangelical wing of the church has other priorities. In the preface of her book, *Desire for God and the Things of God,* Wyndy Corbin Reuschling is perplexed by the fact that evangelicals seem to ignore the social justice ramifications of the gospel message.[3] Why does the mission of the church not explicitly include and encompass social justice? There is an attempt to put an artificial distinction between secular and spiritual aspects of life. Being involved in other people's affairs, especially with regard to social justice matters, is what God expects of the church that is called by his name. Besides the promotion of righteousness and social justice among the needy people in society, involvement in such activities is itself socially and morally formative for those involved.

Diana Butler Bass, and others, note that in the West spirituality and religion have become two distinct things. In that regard, there is need to contend with the fact that it is now normal to hear the talk about the importance of being spiritual but not religious, as if the two are separable. Indeed, Bass observes that it was in the 1990s in the West that Christian vitality was so eroded that it became commonplace to assert that one could be spiritual but not religious. Bass adds that this was akin to "religion-less Christianity," a phrase attributed to the late German Lutheran pastor Dietrich Bonhoeffer (1906–1945) describing the lukewarm church.[4] An attempt to argue for a spirituality devoid of religion just does not work. This reminds me of a wisdom saying among the Kikuyu people-group of Kenya: *Guthura ng'ombe ni*

1. Wolterstorff, *Journey toward Justice*, 70.
2. Grenz, *Pocket Dictionary*, 48.
3. Reuschling, *Desire for God*, xiv-xv.
4. Bass, *People's History of Christianity*, loc. 3694.

guthura kamukwa kayo. A literal translation to English is: "To despise the ox means to despise also a strip of hide from it." Its close equivalent would be: "You cannot have your cake and eat it, too." Despite this insistence that one can be spiritual without being religious, it is possible that this perspective is indicative of the existence of a problem in Christian faith and practice when it comes to social justice.

Thus, an urgent re-examination is needed of how followers of Jesus Christ live out their faith, so that the larger society can come to appreciate the fact that, from a Christian point of view, you can be both religious and spiritual. Reuschling laments that the concept of spirituality has changed, leading some people to conclude that what is important is being spiritual without necessarily being religious. Consequently, borrowing from Wuthnow's view of spirituality in America, Reuschling notes that there has been a significant shift in the understanding of spirituality. This is due primarily to what she describes as a replacement of "a spirituality of dwelling" by the "spirituality of seeking."[5] This phenomenon is related to a growing distrust of religious institutions, among other key contributors to increasing distancing of individuals from "traditional ways of learning about God and interacting with the sacred."[6] This attempt to separate spirituality and religion is evidence of people not wanting to "belong," hence the tendency towards a detachment from ecclesial institutions. This might explain why people are searching for spirituality outside the church so they can be spiritual without being religious.

This lack of commitment to the community of faith may stem from the assumption that spirituality is personal, private, and individualized whereas religion is a more public and corporate expression. But, are spirituality and religion really mutually exclusive? Reuschling explains that spirituality ultimately involves real persons who are "embodied, identifiable, and corporate."[7] These are people actively living out their Christian lives in their dispositions and actions for the good of others.[8] Thus, they are both religious and spiritual. In that sense, according to Reuschling, spirituality is seen as desiring the right things of God while morality is about the right things to desire; namely, justice, righteousness, and mercy.[9] Morality, here, can be interchanged with religion. Thus, spirituality and religion are not mutually exclusive as they are both about people who are living out their faith in real world.

5. Reuschling, *Desire for God*, 4.
6. Reuschling, *Desire for God*, 4.
7. Reuschling, *Desire for God*, 14.
8. Reuschling, *Desire for God*, 14–21.
9. Reuschling, *Desire for God*, 29.

Spirituality and religion are, therefore, inseparable. Thus, as Christians express their love for God through joyful pursuit of God's desires, their spirituality, morality, and religious inclinations are formed. In any case, as Micah 6:8 admonishes, it is through worship that God's people are morally formed through a constant reminder of what God desires of them, which is to practice justice, love kindness, and to walk humbly with God.[10] Once God's desires are known and acted upon by his people, they in turn guide, shape, and provide content for moral formation through practices of justice out of love for God and others. As a result, we are directed toward three areas: the good of others, the practice and formation of social virtues, and the heightening of our moral sensibilities as actors in social contexts.[11]

According to Craig Dykstra and Dorothy Bass, Christian practices help to not only integrate religion and spirituality but also to mutually reinforce the two and influence each other.[12] This view is shared by Reuschling, who notes that it is through Christian practices that our spiritual and ethical commitments are formed and concretized.[13] This takes place in three ways. First, it takes place through forming, training, and orienting us to establish habits conducive to spiritual and moral growth. Second, it extends our beliefs by making them visible to others. Third, practices enable us to resist dominant trends and ideologies that not only co-opt our faith but also derail our faithful living in the world.[14] Religion and spirituality thus become both visible and inseparable. Regrettably, important as Christian practices are to the life of the community of faith by integrating spirituality and religion, these practices are said to be "in trouble," possibly due to our society's insistence on individualism and self.[15]

As it has been discussed above, it is possible to be both spiritual and religious. Any split between the two is detrimental to a holistic ethic that ties together spirituality from morality. That is precisely why the presence of the church is urgently needed in matters touching on social justice in the world today for purposes of bridging this artificial divide. It is in the practice of faith that the voice of the church is heard. That way, Christian orthodoxy and Christian orthopraxis will be able to complement each other, since the two are like two sides of the same coin. It is spirituality and religion in mutual coexistence, since, as James 2:14–26 admonishes, faith without

10. Reuschling, *Desire for God*, 37.

11. Reuschling, *Desire for God*, 37.

12. Dykstra and Bass, "Times of Yearning."

13. Reuschling, *Desire for God*, 53.

14. Reuschling, *Desire for God*, 55–60.

15. Dykstra and Bass, "Times of Yearning," 11.

works is dead. Jordan J. Ballor and Robert Joustra in their edited volume, *The Church's Social Responsibility*, and Noel Castellanos' *Where the Cross Meets the Street* help to show how the church can be actively involved in works of service as part of her mission to the world.[16] Christians can, thus, be faithful witnesses in proclamation and performance of works of service like social justice, both inside the church as well as in the public square.

THE CHURCH AND SOCIAL JUSTICE

Thankfully, the church is waking up to its social responsibilities, and the need of its adherents to be a reliable witness in an increasingly secularized world. It may be a bitter reality that the fastest growth of the church is no longer in the West but in Asia, Latin America, and Africa.[17] It may be correct also to describe Africa in particular as truly "a heartland of the Christian faith."[18] Africa, and indeed the Global South in general, is the new center for Christian vibrancy. James Dunn believes that Pentecostal influence in Latin America and Africa is particularly credited for this phenomenal church growth, including involvement in church missions and a concern for social justice.[19] The Latin-American church is specially credited for its fight against poverty, oppression, and injustice, including addressing the very causes of those systemic injustices.[20] In a sense, therefore, it is the Global South, not the Global North, that is now the nerve of Christian missionary work.

However, there seems to be a ray of hope in the West. The church in the West seems to be waking up to its commitment to social justice as an expression of Christian faith. Ballor and Joustra note that there is "a minor renaissance in thinking about the church," and this offers hope that the church in the Western world can again take its rightful place as a faithful witness in the marketplace of ideas.[21] The church in the West, and particularly Europe, is, therefore, gradually returning to that time when it was not only the center of spiritual vibrancy, but also a key player in sending out Christian workers to the rest of the world. According to Bass, despite the general downward spiral of open expressions of Christian faith in the West, there is a significant

16. Ballor and Joustra, "Introduction," 3; Castellanos, *Where the Cross Meets the Street*.

17. Bediako, *Jesus and the Gospel in Africa*, 3; Johnstone, *Future of the Global Church*, 126–29; Shaw, *Global Awakening*, 11.

18. Bediako, *Jesus and the Gospel in Africa*, 3.

19. Dunn, "Pentecostalism and the Charismatic Movement."

20. Gutiérrez, *We Drink from Our Own Wells*.

21. Ballor and Joustra, "Introduction," 54.

contribution of individual Christians in the twentieth century. Bass further mentions several outstanding figures who have greatly shaped the debate on social justice both in North America and elsewhere. These include Dorothy Day, Dietrich Bonhoeffer, C.S. Lewis, Howard Thurman, Thomas Merton, Oscar Romero, Verna Dozier, Madeleine L'Engle, and Henri Nouwen.[22] There is hope, therefore, that the church in the West is rising to the occasion in championing for social justice as part of its overall mission.

Ballor and Joustra further argue the church has a social responsibility, as indicated by the way it has historically run such programs as schools, hospitals, soup kitchens, and homeless shelters; the church has also ensured that its voice is heard relating to social concerns on the local and international levels.[23] This renewed concern did not begin recently. It is part of church tradition and history. Bass notes that early Christian writings extoled hospitality toward the sick, the poor, travelers, widows, orphans, slaves, prisoners, prostitutes, and the dying. These deeds were not just talked about but actually practiced.[24]

Donald W. Dayton presents a fairly comprehensive review of the history of the church's involvement in social justice, including associated successes and failures. He notes in particular that the social agenda as advanced by the North American church has historically experienced "an ebb-and-flow pattern alternating between periods of creative vitality and periods of stability."[25] Despite all those challenges, it is important to appreciate the steadfastness of the church in its call and commitment to social witness. All that is required is continued rekindling of that fire so that the church can retain its faithful prophetic witness in the world.

Although the church has not always been consistent in its observance of social concerns, God's people have always been expected to adhere to this tradition. The church of today is no different regarding this expectation, because doing so is part of the mission God has called Jesus' disciples to accomplish in society. This vision of the church's responsibility toward society is being recaptured by the church in the West. Indeed, as Ballor and Joustra would argue, the church not only matters for public life, but it also has a social mandate to shape and respond to that responsibility.[26]

Vincent Bacote notes in regard to the church's commitment to social justice that, although there may be some Christians who still question the

22. Bass, *People's History of Christianity*, loc. 3831.

23. Ballor and Joustra, "Introduction," 51.

24. Bass, *People's History of Christianity*, loc. 893.

25. Dayton, *Discovering an Evangelical Heritage*, 122.

26. Ballor and Joustra, "Introduction," 68.

place of social justice as part of Christian mission, times have changed for the better. There is less fear than formerly when the social gospel was dismissed as too worldly, too focused on the earthly dimensions of God's kingdom.[27] Thus, the church's engagement in social justice issues is nowadays a norm. The issue is now such a given that denominations or individual congregations are encouraged to engage in matters of social justice. What matters, therefore, is what mechanisms should be adopted so that such involvement can be seamlessly integrated within the overarching mission of the church. Simply put, it is not a question of "if" the church should be involved, but rather "how" that can be done. That is a great breakthrough and a remarkable milestone in the life of the church.

As an example, Mike Hogeterp has vilified the church in Canada for its past complicity in systemic dehumanization of indigenous peoples through the so-called Doctrine of Christian Discovery.[28] As a result, there has been a "long-standing shrouding of the Good News, and the denial of the fullness of the image of God in Indigenous People."[29] Thankfully, the church has recently joined other partners in engaging in issues relating to indigenous peoples and the age-old oppression meted out against that people-group.[30] Thus, this action by the Canadian Church provides a good example of how God's people can be involved in not only addressing social justice issues, but also how it may be actively involved in dismantling social, cultural, political, and economic systems responsible for subjugating humans to indignities that disrespect the *imago Dei* in humanity.

Thus, the church in Canada has regretted its past perpetration of injustices and has begun to be intentional about doing something about this dark past that has tainted its image. Subsequently, the church has joined the government, itself an equal accomplice in this perpetration of injustice, to offer "words of apology and confession to Indigenous People."[31] It is hoped that those good symbolic words will be followed by action. This is a poignant reminder of the fact that the church should admit where it has erred and begin to right wrongs and promote social justice.

That is the mission of the church and its task in accomplishing the *mission Dei.*

The above case of the church in Canada is a stark reminder that the church in general has been called to not practice a dry religion but to clearly

27. Bacote, "Social Justice and Christian Obedience," loc. 1477.

28. Hogeterp, "Why the Church Must Not Stay Silent," loc. 1125.

29. Hogeterp, "Why the Church Must Not Stay Silent," loc. 1094.

30. Hogeterp, "Why the Church Must Not Stay Silent," loc. 1125.

31. Hogeterp, "Why the Church Must Not Stay Silent," loc. 1149.

demonstrate God's love for humanity and his creation. Whatever the church does, it is important to remember that it is God's representative. Hogeterp reminds us that our worship services are a series of rituals performed in public that present Christ's ministry of reconciliation. This means that church liturgy promotes justice and reconciliation.[32] Toward that end, Hogeterp summarizes this thought very well by implying that God's people cannot afford to abdicate their social responsibility to the society: "for the integrity of liturgy as public service, the church needs to be vocal and active on matters of justice and reconciliation."[33]

A HOLISTIC GOSPEL

Followers of Jesus Christ are referred to as both the salt of the earth and the light of the world (Matt 5:13–16). They are, therefore, agents of the kingdom of God, with the divine mandate of pointing society to what is right, honorable, and good for human society. Richard Stearns points out that being a Christian requires more than a personal and transforming relationship. It also entails a public and transforming relationship with the world.[34] This observation challenges the church to be in the forefront as effective agents of transformation of societies because it possesses a dynamic life that comes from God. That life is the gospel of the kingdom of God that the church has historically proclaimed, or at least has been expected to proclaim. It is what Richard Stearns calls the new world order, since this "gospel itself was born of God's vision of a changed people, challenging and transforming the prevailing values and practices of our world."[35] The church has historically been the carrier of the gospel of the kingdom of God, and societies are expected to be impacted positively and transformed through the subversive nature of this gospel through the agency of God's people, the church.

Although much may have been done to inculcate values of the kingdom into the society as part of *gospeling*, one needs to add that this spreading of the good news is only one part of the church's task. There is need to herald the message of the kingdom through deeds as well. Thus, the two components of *gospeling* and inviting people to receive the news makes the presentation of the gospel more complete. That is what makes the gospel good news, demanding a complete change for its recipients. This is because, as N.T. Wright suggests, something has happened as a result of which the

32. Hogeterp, "Why the Church Must Not Stay Silent," loc. 1108–11.

33. Hogeterp, "Why the Church Must Not Stay Silent," loc. 1114.

34. Stearns, *Hole in Our Gospel*, 2.

35. Stearns, *Hole in Our Gospel*, 2.

world is a different place.[36] There is no point in telling people about God's reign, which Jesus announced in Luke 17:21 was in their midst, without giving them the opportunity to embrace it. Thus, what churches ought to be doing is not only to tell about the reign of God, but to also endeavor to demonstrate in all possible practical ways the actual presence of this kingdom. That is precisely "bringing God into the public square," including working for justice and peace against all odds, against a secularism which would rather see "the church shrink, huddle into a corner, and ultimately disappear altogether."[37]

It is, therefore, not enough to proclaim tenets of Christian belief, whether corporately or individually, without going further into translating those convictions into actual concrete and tangible results evident to all, both in the church as well as outside the four walls of the church. The true mark of a transformed life is seen when emphasis is placed on holistic approaches to doing ministry for purposes of bringing total transformation of individuals, communities, and societies.[38]

If churches want to continue to be relevant in a changing world, they have no choice but to integrate intentionally rigorous philosophy, Christian theology, and sound economics in their thinking about social justice in everyday life situations. This is the case especially when we consider the need for religious ideals and virtues in running businesses in a world bent on undermining the very core foundation of integrity in human relationships. There is need to explore various aspects of liberties and justice with emphasis on Christian moral and ethical perspectives. That way, it will be possible for the church to provide an environment conducive to intense discussion of ideas and issues in social justice. In order to do that, there is need to have faith-rooted organizing. According to Alexia Salvatierra and Peter Heltzel, such organizing is shaped and guided by faith principles and practices for creating just communities and societies.[39] Indeed, the church can demonstrate how faith-rooted Christian values can be harnessed and utilized to bring order to society.

Pope John Paul II's pastoral letter, *Centesimus Annus*, presents a pastoral perspective on what it means to promote justice in society at all levels. This document details social and economic injustices prevalent at the international levels. These injustices have, in turn, especially impacted the poor more than other people. As would be expected in a pastoral letter, the

36. Wright, *Simply Good News*, 16.

37. Wright, *Day the Revolution Began*, loc. 5771.

38. Brown, *Becoming Whole and Holy*.

39. Salvatierra and Heltzel, *Faith-Rooted Organizing*, 9.

Pope pleads with the international community to rise to the occasion and do something about oppressive situations.[40]

In urging society to be virtuous, irrespective of whether such acts produce benefits to people practicing them, Pope John Paul II laments alienation, which makes humanity not recognize in themselves and in others "the value and grandeur of the human person."[41] As a result, humans effectively deprive themselves of the possibility of benefitting from their "humanity and of entering into that relationship of solidarity and communion with others for which God created him."[42] There is need, therefore, for humans to co-operate and assist each other in promoting social justice, for it is in so doing that humanity reflects God's image.

Thus, human effort devoid of God's enabling power to bring about social justice is an exercise in futility. It takes a transformed mind and a changed heart to bring about change in society. That is why Pope John Paul II's contribution in this debate shows how the church can really become an instrument for bringing about justice and righteousness. These virtues are desperately needed for administering justice in the world today. Considering what this document espouses, we are challenged to appreciate that humans are not only created by God and in his image but that they play an important role as co-operators with God in the work of creation.[43]

Likewise, in opposition to the rise in secularism, which, unfortunately, tends to link religion with oppression, Robert Sirico defends the role of spirituality in human progress. He particularly emphasizes the fact that civilizations have survived and flourished throughout history on the foundation of religion.[44] Sirico further cautions religious leaders against shying away from justice matters, such as helping people who are suffering, feeding the hungry, or caring for the poor, on the pretense that the state will meet those needs. He argues, "The church's mission should not be relegated to the role of lobbyist; that deprives the church of the spiritual nourishment that comes from actually performing acts of mercy."[45] The church should therefore be fully involved in addressing human needs and thereby help to build a just society.

40. Paul II, *Centesimus Annus*, 53.
41. Paul II, *Centesimus Annus*, 41.
42. Paul II, *Centesimus Annus*, 41.
43. Paul II, *Centesimus Annus*, 37.
44. Sirico, *Moral Basis for Liberty*, 8.
45. Sirico, *Moral Basis for Liberty*, 29.

CONTEMPORARY EXAMPLES

As the twenty-first century progresses, we see the church becoming increasingly engaged in contemporary debates about social justice issues. This includes a re-examination of systems that are responsible for either promoting or stifling human dignity and justice in society. That active involvement in the cause of social justice is seen as pivotal to the very core of the mission of the church. The Acton Institute, a Christian policy think-tank, is one example of how the church is actively engaged in influencing policy decisions that touch on justice-related issues in society. The Acton Institute seeks to promote integration of Christian moral values and human freedoms both in the United States and in the rest of the world. This organization is especially active in providing training to Christian leaders and business people on how to promote free markets, economic justice, and human rights. Given its mission of promoting a free, virtuous, and humane society, the Acton Institute organizes conferences and similar forums in order to teach the advantages of limited governments and free markets. Emphasis is particularly placed on the need to embrace and promote justice for the common good. Thus, this organization inculcates a sense of fostering an understanding of the need for a harmonious intersection of faith, liberty, and justice in free societies aspiring to have vibrant economies.

The American church has tried to make great strides in mainstreaming social justice in her programs of activities. One of the most remarkable initiatives in this respect has been the launching of post-civil rights social movements that have sensitized Christians to the need for addressing social justice. One such initiative is the Christian Community Development Association (CCDA). CCDA is a shining example of intentional contemporary Christian initiative aimed at promoting social justice and human dignity for the kingdom of God. The beginnings of this organization in the 1960s can be traced to the activities of John Perkins, an African-American Christian from the state of Mississippi. CCDA was born out of Perkin's desire to turn his tragedies and suffering under the hands of brutal police beatings and torture during the Civil Rights Movement activities into something positive.

As a result, according to Soong-Chan Rah and Gary VanderPol, John Perkins translated his story into a movement. That is how CCDA was born. Perkins was intent on changing the world by changing individual lives through holistic evangelism. He felt a call to incarnate himself into his community so as effectively to "minister to the poor and the marginalized."[46] As a Christian organization, CCDA is deeply committed to promoting social

46. Rah and VanderPol, *Return to Justice*, 504–46.

justice among the marginalized and, especially, the poor. It inspires, trains, and connects Christians to bear witness to the kingdom of God by reclaiming and restoring under-resourced communities. The result is holistically restored communities, with Christians fully engaged in the process of transformation. Over the years, CCDA has held training sessions and conferences for purposes of sharing the vision of serving the poor and the marginalized members of society, especially those in urban areas. It is through CCDA's activities that previously ignored aspects of church ministry experience such as service to the poor, community development, racial reconciliation, civil rights, and redistribution of resources have been successfully moved into the mainstream of evangelicalism.[47]

CCDA has espoused eight principles that powerfully propel this organization in the quest for the promotion of social justice. These are:

1. Relocation, involving change agents investing in the community by living among the people they are serving. This is incarnation with Jesus being a good example of one who not only "became flesh and blood," but also relocated "into the neighborhood" of humanity (John 1:14).
2. Reconciliation of people to God and of people to one another.
3. Redistribution of resources as part of justice.
4. Leadership development and the promotion of local leadership as a long-term investment for sustainable development.
5. Listening to the community by taking into account the thoughts, hopes, dreams, ideas, and aspirations of the community. That is done so that communities can find solutions to their problems, not so others can impose solutions on them.
6. A church-based approach, with the understanding that the community of God's people is well-placed to promote human dignity.
7. A holistic approach that goes beyond evangelism and discipleship. This approach addresses the complex needs that define a whole person, that is social, economic, political, emotional, physical, judicial, educational, and familial needs.
8. Empowerment of people to meet their needs. That involves passing the baton by not doing for people what they can do themselves so they can be proud of what they are doing on their own.

Communities adopting CCDA's model of holistic development have experienced great transformation. Mae Elise Cannon gives the example of

47. Rah and VanderPol, *Return to Justice*, 627.

Lawndale in the West Side of Chicago, Illinois, as a case in point of such communities that have experienced tangible transformation. This neighborhood has experienced social transformation through the catalysis of Lawndale Community Church. Since its establishment in 1975, this church has initiated multifaceted development initiatives that have addressed diverse community needs. Prime among these ministries are housing, job training, restoration of ex-prisoners, security, health, and programs of activities for children.[48] These are true acts of justice that meet real needs of real people in real settings.

As Bass would put it, "[j]ustice is not a metaphor" but a tangible reality that all humanity must come to terms with.[49] It is one thing to talk about what justice ought to be. It is another thing altogether to demonstrate with deeds what justice really looks like. Rah and VanderPol attest to this contribution of Lawndale Community Church in modeling how church ought to be involved actively in promoting social justice through words and deed. Thus, "Lawndale became an exemplar church for the CCDA."[50] Their holistic approach to doing ministry in a poor and disadvantaged neighborhood is an example worth of emulation by other Christian churches and denominations.

COLLABORATIVE CONFRONTATION OF SOCIAL INJUSTICES

The church should address social injustices by forging appropriate collaborative efforts. But in order to do this effectively, there is need to first understand the intricacy of this problem. In his book, *The Prophetic Imagination*, Walter Brueggemann discusses the application of the concept of the kingdom of God in the church ministry. He specifically encourages the church to be actively engaged in "prophetic imagination" by participating in what he refers to as "the one prophetic ministry of formation and reformation of alternative community."[51] For instance, with reference to Jesus' announcement of his ministry in Luke 4:18–19, Brueggemann observes that Jesus harshly criticized agents of the present order that perpetuated the oppressive and unjust system that was ripe for dismantling. As a result, Jesus declared the dawn of the new age of the kingdom of God. In view

48. Cannon, *Social Justice Handbook*, 116–17.

49. Bass, *People's History of Christianity*, loc. 3950.

50. Rah and VanderPol, *Return to Justice*, 587.

51. Brueggemann, *Prophetic Imagination*, 4.

of this proclamation, Brueggemann summarizes this annunciation of Jesus' ministry and its far-reaching implications for today's church:

> His message was to the poor, but others kept them poor and benefitted from their poverty. He addressed the captives (which means bonded salves), but others surely wanted that arrangement unchanged. He named the oppressed, but there are never oppressed without oppressors.[52]

Walter Brueggemann implies that, whereas it is important to identify people who are oppressed, we must go further to understand who are the oppressors and what are the oppressive systems that support the practice. Such an appraisal of the intricate web of systems that are associated with social oppression is necessary if we are going to be effective in addressing social injustices that have led to the perpetuation of the indignity of humans. The call for the dismantling of oppressive systems that distort the work of the kingdom of God among God's creation was just as urgent in Jesus' day as it is today. The church is expected to do what the master did. Certainly, being involved in championing social-structural change is one of the roles the church is called upon to undertake. The mission of the church is not only to herald the arrival of the new age of the kingdom, but it is also to be part of the agency for bringing about that change.

A candid discussion of the kingdom of God and the church has to include the idea of reconciliation. That is because it is the church that has been called to be God's agent of reconciliation. The church ought to be preoccupied with doing holistic ministry to the entire creation and to reconcile it to the creator. Obviously, this task may not, and will not, achieve the fullness of the expectation of what the ideal kingdom of God will look like at the Eschaton. This is why there is this view of the kingdom "now" and "not-yet," the latter being what will be achieved in the future. N.T. Wright helps to put this idea in the right perspective:

> The final kingdom, when it comes, will be the free gift of God, a massive act of grace and new creation. But we are called to build for the kingdom. Like craftsmen working on a great cathedral, we have each been given instructions about the particular stone we are to spend our lives carving, without knowing or being able to guess where it will take its place within the grand design. We are assured, by the words of Paul and by Jesus's resurrection as the launch of that new creation, that the work we do is not in vain.[53]

52. Brueggemann, *Prophetic Imagination*, 84.

53. Wright, *Surprised by Scripture*, 106.

And recently, a friend succinctly captured the essence of the workings of the kingdom of God this way:

> The kingdom of God on earth today means that the values and virtues of the world to come are breaking into our contemporary culture, offering a glimpse of the way things will be when the king returns to live among us. The church serves as the agent of the kingdom and individual congregations, ideally, as outposts of the kingdom in their neighborhoods. As kingdom citizens, when it comes to the attitude of our hearts in relating to the world around us, there is but one guiding principle: does it reflect the values of the kingdom and the character of the king?

In today's world, addressing social justice issues, with a view to improving the standards of living of communities and society in general, requires joint collaboration of various stakeholders, including public-private partnerships, nonprofit organizations, and civil society and community groups. Such inclusiveness is crucial because no single individual or organization can improve society singlehandedly. As Charles Marsh would argue, Christian workers must be humble enough to recognize efforts of other entities, most of whom may not be Christians, and yet are doing the same work of the kingdom.[54]

There is therefore need to engage in genuine partnerships devoid of arrogance, based on the assumption that Christians are not the only ones involved in shaping communities. It is therefore prudent to appreciate the crucial role of collaborative ventures between church and state that entail partnerships with certain government organs on social justice. Secular governments, on their part, should endeavor to provide an enabling environment for social justice and human flourishing, but not attempt to do what individuals and communities can do by, and for, themselves.[55] The principle of subsidiarity explains how larger and more complex organizations like governments should not be allowed to do what can be done as well by smaller, simpler, and more centralized entities. Subsidiarity is the principle behind advocacy for limited government and personal freedom, the very antithesis of centralization and bureaucracy that are characteristic of the Welfare State.[56]

Such collaboration between communities and the state is crucial in advancing the cause of social justice. This is the case because, as it has been noted by Nicholas P. Wolterstorff, governments or state organs have a

54. Marsh and Perkins, *Welcoming Justice*, 100–102.

55. Piedra, *Natural Law*, 159.

56. Bosnich, "Principle of Subsidiarity," 9.

God-assigned task of exercising governance over the public to curb injustice and to encourage justice.[57] It is, therefore, the duty of relevant state organs to use the instruments in their powers to ensure justice prevails. As Um and Buzzard note, although today's institutional church may not have a juridical authority in the public square, this does not mean that the church has to stay on the periphery.[58]

Um and Buzzard argue further that, indeed, the church has a civic responsibility to the city with regard to such issues such as education, ministry to the poor, alleviation of social injustice, and the arts. That is, the Christian responsibility of acting in mercy and in engaging "our community with deeds of social justice."[59] The church would, therefore, be wise to work alongside state institutions, since the two institutions are not competing against each other, but rather are complementary to one another for the common good.

In his book, *We Drink from Our Own Wells*, Gustavo Gutiérrez discusses in detail how promotion of the gospel of liberation in Latin America by local people provides a lesson on how the church can involve its congregants in shaping their communities. It is a demonstration of how Christians can individually and corporately deal with their own social justice issues.[60] Any success in addressing social justice needs can only be measured by the extent to which local people are involved, so that the results can be sustainable and become truly owned by the people themselves. Samuel Wells and Marcia A. Owen show a case in point of broad inclusiveness where forums, like vigils for victims of violent crimes in Durham, North Carolina, are convened. In such events, stakeholder participation is both encouraged and demonstrated in very practical ways.[61]

Engagement in strategies for addressing social justice issues for purposes of community building begins with the recognition that something is wrong, that people are suffering, and, therefore, that something needs to be done about their situation. However, easy as this might sound, the sheer magnitude of issues can easily lead to paralysis, despair, and cynicism. These negative emotions can often deincentivize doing anything, especially when one is too careful not to "do the wrong thing in the wrong place at the wrong time in the wrong way for the wrong reasons."[62]

57. Wolterstorff, "Contours of Justice," 199.

58. Um and Buzzard, *Why Cities Matter*, 89.

59. Um and Buzzard, *Why Cities Matter*, 89–90.

60 Gutiérrez, *We Drink from Our Own Wells.*

61. Wells and Owen, *Living without Enemies*, 59.

62. Wells and Owen, *Living without Enemies*, 22.

THE CHURCH AND SOCIAL JUSTICE: WHITHER THE WAY FORWARD?

The church is expected to be engaged actively in holistic ministry, including involvement in social ministries. Peter Wagner puts heavy emphasis on the dual role that the church plays in accomplishing her mission: the cultural mandate and the evangelistic mandate.[63] Ordinarily, the church tends to emphasize one at the expense of the other. On one hand, the evangelistic mandate is elevated based on a misconstrued conviction that the Great Commission is primarily and explicitly about verbal proclamation as well as spiritual concerns.[64] On the other hand, where the cultural mandate and social concerns are emphasized, stress is laid on social action that addresses oppressive social structures as well as social service that aims at meeting the immediate and long-term needs in society. In that regard, John R. Stott makes it clear that the church has "no liberty either to concentrate on evangelism to the exclusion of social concern or to make social activism a substitute for evangelism."[65]

Although spiritual and social concerns are legitimately part of the ministry of the church, neither should be emphasized at the expense of the other. The two are not mutually exclusive, but complementary. The kingdom of God, which the church is called to herald, is a holistic one. It is God's reign in and among his people as well as in the entire creation. It involves a demonstration of God's tender love and care in the creation he so loved that he gave Jesus Christ for its total re-creation. Therefore, an artificial separation of the cultural mandate from the evangelistic mandate is a too narrow compartmentalized view of the nature of the gospel. It fails to capture the larger picture of God's activity within creation.

Jessica Driesenga states it very well when she laments that Christian posture toward the world is like there is an either/or decision to be made: either to choose to be part of the world or separate from it for the sake of the gospel.[66] Of course, Christians have no choice between the two, because the church is in the world to change and influence it positively for God and his kingdom. Thus, such a change need not be labeled *spiritual* or *physical*. H. Richard Niebuhr notes in his works, *Christ and Culture* and *The kingdom of God in America*, that the kingdom of God that the church advances involves a holistic transformation of all aspects of human life, culturally and politically.

63. Wagner, *Church Growth*.

64. Sider, *Good News and Good Works*; Sider et al., *Churches That Make a Difference*.

65. Stott, *Christian Mission*, 25–26.

66. Driesenga, "Pearl and a Leaven," loc. 606.

There is a need to address structural changes and societal transformation so that the root causes of these social issues can be dealt with at their core.

Such transaction ought to be the focus in church's efforts to relate with the needy sections of society. This explains the importance of going beyond mere relief and individual development to address community development and structural changes required in order to deal with endemic causes of social problems. That is holistic ministry that can only take place in a holistic church.[67] Indeed, as the title of this book by Sider, Olson, and Unruh suggests, such a holistic approach is the way to ensure that churches make a difference in their local communities. The church has an obligation to address social justice issues and, most importantly, the causes of those problems. However, in its enthusiasm, the church needs to be careful not to sell its soul by sacrificing the very core of its identity, which also defines its mission. It is with this understanding that Kevin N. Flatt admonishes the church to be extremely careful not to be a captive to ideological forces only superficially connected to Scripture and the tradition of Christian social thought, but instead nurture what he calls "a robust spiritual life and a thoroughly biblical social witness."[68]

Social justice and human rights are inseparable since they both feed into each other. It is actually right to note that human rights can be regarded as rights entitled to anyone who fulfills the criteria of being human, irrespective of their capabilities or limitations. Thus, Wolterstorff notes that even impaired people still retain human nature and therefore are entitled to human rights.[69] Wolterstorff adds that there are two categories of rights: the rights that one has, other things being equal (defined as *prima facie*) and the rights that one has, all things considered (defined as *ultima facie*).[70] It should be noted that Judeo-Christian view of human rights as an aspect of social justice is predicated upon the understanding that human beings bear the image of God. This means that irrespective of one's capacity to function in a certain way, or despite one's disabilities, each individual still bears the image of God. Thus, Wolterstorff advocates a nature-resemblance account of the image of God instead of the secular traditional capacities-resemblance or role-resemblance accounts. This means that human rights are not based

67. Sider et al., *Churches That Make a Difference*, 15.

68. Flatt, "Historical Epilogue," loc. 1659, 1667.

69. Wolterstorff, *Journey toward Justice*, 135.

70. Wolterstorff, *Journey toward Justice*, 131–32.

on human nature but rather, from a theistic point of view, human beings resemble God with respect to their human nature.[71]

Esther D. Reed notes that the subject of human rights occupies a very important part in modern political thought. In view of that, Christians have no choice but to defend those rights as a response to "God's graciousness toward humankind."[72] This commitment is based on assumptions about "God's preserving providence in ordering creaturely realities to their proper ends."[73] In addition, Reed contends that human rights have to be understood within a given context; because "right" has to have limits, as it is not "primarily a liberty or zone of non-interference that sets one individual apart from another but that which is owed to a person by virtue of his or her existence within divine providence."[74]

This explains why participation and decision-making regarding promotion of individual and community needs are paramount. Hence there is a need for finding milestones that the church has reached in promoting social justice in its respective areas of ministry. In this regard, what JJMC is doing is a justice undertaking, which is clearly part of the mission of the church. Attributing the slogan "No justice, No Jesus" to Stanley Hauerwas, David E. Fitch and Geoff Holsclaw clarify that "the church is a social manifestation of God's Lordship over the world in and through Jesus Christ" and therefore "a foretaste of God's kingdom in the world" and a sign of God's justice working in the whole world.[75] If there is no justice in our lives, then Jesus is not present, either. The proclamation of God's salvation and addressing injustice in society are inseparable, since anyone truly redeemed by God cannot help but be involved in justice issues. Individual conversion and reconciliation in the world are related.[76]

N.T. Wright discusses the issue of kingdom versus the cross. These two represent different strands of Christians. Each competes for attention, yet they seem to disagree on what God accomplished through Jesus Christ. Thus, we have "cross Christians" and "kingdom Christians." The former emphasizes the agenda of saving souls as the focus of Jesus' death. The latter emphasize the social gospel agenda.[77] This discussion is akin to the evangelistic versus cultural mandate debates in missiology. Wright says the two

71. Wolterstorff, *Journey toward Justice*, 137.
72. Reed, *Ethics of Human Rights*, 2–3.
73. Reed, *Ethics of Human Rights*, 3.
74. Reed, *Ethics of Human Rights*, 3.
75. Fitch and Holsclaw, *Prodigal Christianity*, loc. 4059.
76. Fitch and Holsclaw, *Prodigal Christianity*, loc. 4059.
77. Wright, *How God Became King*, 157.

views are, in a sense, two sides of the same coin. Each of the two apparently differing perspectives show what Jesus accomplished, and the difference is only for purposes of conceptualizing the ministry of Jesus and his mandate on the earth. That explains why Eugene Cho is emphatic that no Christian ministry can compartmentalize the physical and spiritual in pursuit of justice and of the kingdom of God.[78] It is not a question of choosing between trellis and the vine. Both are important, since they not only complement each other, but they also need each other and, therefore, must be taken care of if the full dynamics of the kingdom of God are to be experienced. Churches and Christian ministries have no choice but to ensure that their approaches to ministries are holistic, practical, realistic, and transformational in their outcomes.

Paying special attention to ministry approaches among the poor and people on the margins of society, Noel Castellanos notes that there are four components that make a Christian ministry successful in addressing the holistic needs of the people to whom they are ministering. He calls those components "pillars" of helping to do what he calls "the cross meeting the street." They are, in his opinion, important ingredients that enable one to "effectively minister in a vulnerable neighborhood in a way that is truly biblical."[79]

Castellanos' first pillar is proclamation and formation, which involves not only announcing the good news, but also allowing this gospel message to be spiritually forming and transformative in a person's life. Second is the demonstration of compassion, where the gospel story is enacted in everyday life through acts of mercy like Jesus did during his earthly ministry. Third is restoration and development, where acts of mercy are not just aimed at addressing immediate physical needs, but also look to the long-term aspects of life that ensure sustainability. The fourth pillar is the confrontation of injustice, in which effort is made to deal with not just symptoms of injustice, but also its very causes. This includes dealing with endemic oppressive systems that perpetuate injustice, as well as promoting advocacy on policy issues that target the very root causes of systemic injustices in the society.[80] All four pillars are joined together by a common thread of incarnation which, in a sense, is an appeal to Christians to immerse themselves in social justice issues and fully identify with those affected.[81] Toward that end, Richard J. Mouw recommends Christians to be "deeply involved in policies and

78. Cho, *Overrated*, loc. 424, 447.

79. Castellanos, *Where the Cross Meets the Street*, loc. 880.

80. Castellanos, *Where the Cross Meets the Street*, loc. 1128–1907.

81. Castellanos, *Where the Cross Meets the Street*, loc. 1750.

practices relating to concern for the poor," including developing policy proposals and discussing them with individuals possessing relevant expertise.[82]

SOCIAL JUSTICE BEYOND THE CHURCH

From the foregoing, it is clear that the church is trying her best to address social justice concerns as part of her ministry to the world. However, this has not been easy-going. It is interesting to look at the church's ambivalence towards embracing social justice matters, especially in urban areas. Over the years, the American church has at one point embraced the city, later shunned the city, and, lately, again embraced the city, so far as social justice issues are concerned. Rah and VanderPol call this a journey from Jerusalem to Babylon that comprises "a complicated relationship with the city."[83] The trend, therefore, has been that any time there would be an optimistic view of the larger society, that would automatically translate into optimism about the city.[84]

Accordingly, Rah and VanderPol argue that Colonial American Christians anticipated cities in the New World would be cities on a hill, the new Jerusalem. It is important to note, however, that, strictly speaking, this situation only applied to Puritan Christians in Colonial New England and not to every Christian in the whole of Colonial America. Nevertheless, Rah and VanderPol point out that this optimism faded with changing urban demographics, and urban decay that made cities "dangerous places." The result was flight from "Babylon" to the safe-havens of the suburbs. In recent times, things have changed. With suburbanites returning to the cities, and thereby contributing to gentrification, the suburban church has now promoted the mission back to the city. The American suburban church, or New Jerusalem, has become an outpost for evangelizing Babylon, the down-town. Thus, these transplanted suburbanites envision themselves as "bringing the heavenly city of Jerusalem from the suburbs to the city."[85] As much as this move is aimed at evangelizing the city, Rah and VanderPol offer a critique of this approach because it only makes things worse. The trend is actually displacing populations who can now no longer afford to pay rent or buy houses in these gentrified areas. This move is on the whole counterproductive in that it runs contrary to the very tenets of the claims of a holistic gospel, which is about "restoring persons and communities to wholeness marked by *shalom*."[86]

82. Mouw, "Carl Henry Was Right," loc. 548.
83. Rah and VanderPol, *Return to Justice*, 392.
84. Rah and VanderPol, *Return to Justice*, 392.
85. Rah and VanderPol, *Return to Justice*, 469.
86. Reuschling, *Desire for God*, 33.

Outside of the church, the global community is equally concerned about cities and the negative consequences of urbanization. The United Nations, in particular, has listed seventeen Sustainable Development Goals (SDGs) that stipulate the need for taking action to address economic and social development issues facing the world in the twenty-first century. The goals address a wide variety of issues that touch on human development, including socio-cultural aspects, human health, and environmental stewardship and sustainability.

All these goals have one thing in common: the promotion of social inclusion. This is not surprising, since the United Nations is a global organization whose primary mandate is the promotion of harmony among its member states. Goal number eleven needs special mention here, in that it addresses issues relevant to cities and urban areas like the neighborhood in which this study is focused. This goal is particularly emphatic about the need to tackle issues affecting poor urban neighborhoods that are in dire need for improved services. This goal has a number of targets relevant to social justice that are expected to be met by 2030. The targets include access to adequate, safe and affordable housing and related basic services. Other targets include upgrading of slums and access to safe, affordable, accessible and sustainable transport systems. The targets place emphasis on improving road safety, especially among those in vulnerable situations, namely women, children, and persons with disabilities. One provision in these targets is the need for enhanced inclusiveness and participatory human settlement planning and management that promotes integrated policies toward inclusion.

These United Nations SDGs address pertinent social-justice related matters that the church would do well to adopt, as well as institute mechanisms for addressing them. The Diocese of Southern Ohio of the Episcopal Church, whose ecclesial jurisdiction includes the city of Columbus, has created a fund that provides grants to those members who would like to do development projects in tandem with any one or several of the UN Sustainable Development Goals. This is a very encouraging gesture, and hopefully other churches and denominations will emulate this fine example.

The need for socially just cities is something that cannot be overemphasized. Franziska Schreiber and Alexander Carius are emphatic on the need for an inclusive city that is positioned to promote social diversity and cohesion. These factors are crucial social justice components for a city that is intent on giving its citizens a sense of belonging by deliberately addressing the unique urban "socioeconomic polarization and spatial segregation" challenges.[87] Inclusivity is a theme that recurs in the United Nations Sus-

87. Schreiber and Carius, "Inclusive City," loc. 6989.

tainable Development Goals. Unless there is appreciation for the need for all humans to work together for the common good, nothing will be achieved. When this perspective is applied to reconciliation and justice as advocated by the church, the same answer keeps recurring. On its part, the church needs to embrace inclusivity so that it can employ effective teamwork to accomplish its mission.

Christena Cleveland discusses this point in her book, *Disunity in Christ*. She shows how sometimes the church body is disunited in its mission for social justice. Such internal exclusiveness is outright counterintuitive to the very tenets that social justice is meant to promote. She laments, for instance, about how minority members of a Christian group may not be included among the valuable members of the all-inclusive *we*. Rather, they are relegated to the status of *them*, that is, subordinate "others" and second-class citizens. In that case, such a minority group is "bound to be dissatisfied." They may feel explicitly welcomed but implicitly excluded and disempowered.[88] The church of the twenty-first century has no choice but to be united internally as it endeavors to be the light of the world. Inclusiveness both among God's people, as well as with those not yet in the fold, is not optional. Inclusiveness in promoting social justice is part of the mission of the church.

Whether in secular or in sacred platforms, the church has come to realize that God has a stake in what happens in human society. The church has also come to terms with the fact that humans are God's image bearers and, hence, it needs an appreciation of the great role that it has in bringing change to our social institutions and human societies. This realization, therefore, places a great responsibility on the church to ensure that Christians live up to God's expectations as his ambassadors. Obviously, as human beings, we are limited in what we can do. However, we should not be deterred from doing what is within our ability. We have the capacity to participate in carrying out the cultural mandate to organize and sustain the created order, which includes the human institutions responsible for administering justice. Humans are endowed with the capacity to choose moral ends, to grow, to exercise responsible freedom, and to act as God's moral agents. According to Genesis 1 and 2 we are God's cocreators and stewards of his created order.

Although human beings are laden with sin, which identifies them with the fallen nature of the created order, they are, nevertheless, expected to live as holy people who reflect God's image. Promotion of that uprightness is what the church is called to champion as God's agents. That is the reason

88. Cleveland, *Disunity in Christ*, 147, 167.

why a commitment to justice is so important. It is, essentially, God's attempt to use his co-creators through the agency of the church to deal with sin and resulting alienation. This is what reconciliation looks like. That is, reconciliation is not just between humans and God, but also between and among humans, as well as between humans and creation. This is what it means to execute justice, which brings salvation and ultimately union with God.[89] This is the mission the church is carrying out in the society.

CONCLUSION

The church cannot escape from its calling to promote God's justice in the world. Through the church, the kingdom of God is breaking forth in the world through acts of social justice. According to David E. Fitch and Geoff Holsclaw, that is the nature of the gospel; it is the kingdom whereby "God in Christ has already begun making the world right" through the church because it is impossible to "proclaim God's salvation in our neighborhoods and ignore injustice as if it is unrelated."[90] Thus, as much as the kingdom of God is not geo-political but spiritual, it should not be construed that this spiritual kingdom is non-materialistic and ethereal.[91] There is a sense in which God's people are expected to not only be heralds of the good news of the kingdom, but also to embody this kingdom as its agents. In that case, works of social justice is one powerful way through which the church is able to demonstrate God's reign in human societies.

Today's church is called to partner with God in his mission of restoration of the whole creation to himself. This task is charged on all God's people, those who are willing to jump on God's project of restoration. Wright calls this operation God's rescue mission, a task initially given to Israel through Abraham and now being undertaken and implemented by the church following the restorative accomplishment by God in and through Jesus Christ.[92] It is a project of restoring all things as God originally intended, and that includes, although it is not limited to, social justice, which focuses largely upon human conditions that impede humans from not only being effective as God's imagers, but also from being active agents of reconciling the whole creation to God.

Paul calls this the project of equipping saints for the work of ministry (Eph 4:12), a task to which the church is called. Indeed, as Wright has

89. Spohn, *Go and Do Likewise*, 108–12.

90. Fitch and Holsclaw, *Prodigal Christianity*, loc. 3891.

91. Reuschling, "Christian Ethical Commitments," 214.

92. Wright, *Case for the Psalms*.

argued, what Jesus accomplished by dying on the cross was not only to deal with the sins of humanity, but it was also a way of commissioning Christian believers to a new vocation as a royal priesthood mandated to restore and reconcile all of God's creation.[93] Reuschling says that the justice Christians are to do is informed by God's concern for all creation, including "making things right, naming evil, restoring what has been broken and lost—restoring persons and communities to wholeness marked by *shalom*."[94] This is the heart of the mission of the church, God's ambassadors of reconciliation.

It is important to understand that addressing social justice issues, especially in a poor urban neighborhood like the Community of Kimball Farms, is, itself, a political issue. Doing so is also liturgical, since this is part of what the church is expected to do as part of worship. Liturgy [*leitourgia*] is a political term that implies worship as well as a public work or service done for the benefit of the community.[95] Within the context of the kingdom of God, such service may include works of social justice.

No wonder M.W. Stamm is emphatic that liturgical Christian worship ought to reflect a biblical vision of justice and love for the whole world and must not rationalize injustice.[96] The church is called to be God's representative on matters of the kingdom, and it is therefore imperative that followers of Jesus Christ take this charge seriously. The church is doing this, and it is hoped that more will be accomplished in the coming days.

That way, as Robert J. Suderman puts it, the church will have succeeded in being the sacrament of God's multidimensional grace. The church will, thus, become that "visible community of Christ where the presence of God's grace can be seen, touched, and experienced," a truly "invitational and hospitable place where those seeking and experiencing life in God may come and live out God's mission with the brothers and sisters of the community and together in the larger world."[97]

In chapter 4, we tell the story of how the project was accomplished. It focuses on the design of the project, the procedure of gathering information, and the assessment methods and procedures. It also includes the research context and the participants in the survey. All that is discussed so as to meet the purpose of this project which was to discover how JJMC influences the local community for the kingdom of God.

93. Wright, *Day the Revolution Began*.

94. Reuschling, *Desire for God*, 33.

95. Stamm, "Liturgy and Worship," 492.

96. Stamm, "Liturgy and Worship," 492.

97. Suderman, "Reflections on Anabaptist Ecclesiology," 158.

Chapter 4

Design, Procedure, and Assessment

The purpose of this project was to discover how J. Jireh Ministries Church of Columbus, Ohio, influences the local community for the kingdom of God. Our goal is to establish if this church is fulfilling its calling to be God's ambassador of reconciliation in establishing the kingdom of God. Second, this study is intent on discovering the extent to which the church impacts the people it is serving. JJMC is, therefore, taken as a case study on the role of the church as a signpost of the kingdom of God. In addition, JJMC is used as an example of practical engagement of the church as a facilitator of the kingdom of God. The study focuses on how JJMC incorporates social justice concerns within its ministry to present a holistic vision of the kingdom of God. Six project goals were set out to guide this project:

- **Project Goal 1:** To discover participants' understanding of the ministries of JJMC in their community.
- **Project Goal 2:** To discover the motivations of participants' involvement in JJMC.
- **Project Goal 3:** To discover how participants have been personally impacted by JJMC.
- **Project Goal 4:** To discover how JJMC has impacted the local community.

- **Project Goal 5:** To discover how participants experience the presence of God through the presence/ministry of JJMC.
- **Project Goal 6:** To discover participants' insights on important social issues that need to be addressed in this community.

The design of this project involves constructing a survey using a questionnaire that had both quantitative as well as qualitative questions to elicit information from a random sample of respondents. Results of the survey were then collated and analyzed one goal at a time. The order of their prominence is as follows: Goal 1, Goal 5, Goal 4, Goal 2, Goal 3, and Goal 6. Details of this outcome are discussed fully in chapter 5. Thereafter, relationships and correlations of the findings were reported with a view of interpreting the mass of data generated by the study, which enabled the writing of the final report.

The study discovered that JJMC has indeed played a significant role as a true signpost of the kingdom of God in Kimball Farms, Ohio. However, despite that general overview, data and information from the field pointed out that some programs and activities were more impactful than others. Therefore, the research findings are recommending a process of "project thinning" so as to help make JJMC more effective in its ministry to the community of Kimball Farms. That will, in the end, help to strengthen Christian witness and impact on the people that live in that neighborhood where this project is based. Details of that analysis and recommendations are found in chapter 6.

CONTEXT

JJMC is located in a poor neighborhood where residents face numerous social, economic, political, and economic challenges. This church exists to not only serve its congregants but also to engage in outreach to the local community. The creed of this church sums up its role in this community in a brochure: "We are the *ekklesia*, the 'called-out ones' of God, and we are to be the prophetic voice and the prophetic presence of Jesus Christ. Our vocation is to enforce the rule and reign of God in the earth." This creed spells out expressly what JJMC stands for and its catalytic role in bringing the reality of the impact of the kingdom of God into the community it serves. The tenets of this church, as expressed in that creed, are reinforced by its purpose statement which reads as follows: "We are developing brick and mortar in order to develop flesh and blood. We develop communities and people." That statement sums up what JJMC does. It reflects a true theology in practice, and a vivid demonstration of the marriage between Christian orthodoxy and orthopraxis.

For some time, the neighborhood where JJMC is located has had no identity. It was generally referred to simply as *South of Main* because of its geographical location. However, through the efforts of JJMC, this neighborhood now is named the Community of Kimball Farms. This new name is a tribute to its rich history of agriculture-related activities. Although this step was taken recently, it is hoped that it will trigger a process of healing that will culminate in restoration of fortunes that this neighborhood has lost over the years. JJMC is proudly associated with this neighborhood as it actively engages in the lives of local residents in all forms of spiritual, social, economic, and political activities.

In this predominantly African-American neighborhood, human brokenness is manifested in different forms. It is an area that has historically experienced social and economic injustices due to past utilitarian-driven policy decisions that have had adverse impacts on the local community. For some time, JJMC has been working in partnership with other like-minded organizations, both ecclesial and non-ecclesial. Such collaborations have been forged so that synergies accruing from such working relationships can be effectively channeled toward addressing the social justice issues of this area. This research project therefore endeavors to discover the extent to which JJMC was able to practice the ministry of presence with a view to offering a prophetic voice of hope in order to help facilitate a restoration of justice, righteousness, and reconciliation.

PARTICIPANTS

This is an action-oriented research project with no pretense of objectivity. In such studies, a specific action is expected that corresponds to the expected outcome of the study in question. There was, therefore, an intentional selection of respondents. The goal was to generate information and data that would help to answer the questions laid out at the beginning of the study. Survey participants were a mixture of genders and ages from the targeted neighborhood.

Individuals identified as potential respondents had to fulfill a number of criteria. They had to be at least eighteen years of age. There needed to be a good mix of males and females. They had to have either lived in or associated with the neighborhood of Kimball Farms for some time, even if that period was less than a year. They had to have had an association with JJMC. The pool was composed of both Christians and non-Christians. The participants included members and non-members of JJMC. Some of the respondents filled out the questionnaire online and independently. Others participated in face-to-face interviews, and their responses were entered into the questionnaire. Out of forty potential respondents identified and who were given questionnaires to complete, twenty-nine responded as participants.

PROCEDURE AND ASSESSMENT

The study had two goals. First, it would fulfill Ashland Theological Seminary's doctoral program's requirement for a practical ministry-oriented project. Second, it would generate enough interest on the part of church workers who are keen on seeing the church play its rightful role in society as an ambassador of the kingdom of God. It was not easy for me to identify a topic. Many different possibilities were considered as I tried to focus on an appropriate study.

Amidst all considerations, one thing was clear: I wanted to do something related to the church, its role in society, and how the kingdom of God is manifested in society through the agency of the church. I had already identified a locality and a church in Columbus, Ohio, I wanted to use as a "laboratory" for testing the influence of the church on the local community. The bulk of the time was spent in shaping and narrowing the focus for purposes of clarity, specificity, and ease in doing the project. Finally, a project proposal was written and approved and this helped me execute this project.

When this project was initially conceived and a proposal developed, plans were to choose select projects, programs, and activities within JJMC with a view to subjecting them to detailed research on their impact on the local community. However, after consulting with the field advisor, and upon careful assessment of the facts on the ground, it was considered prudent not to limit respondents to giving their views on select ministries of JJMC. Instead, focus shifted to letting the respondents communicate their story and tell what ministry programs had the greatest impact on their lives, as well as upon the lives of members of the local community. Thus, respondents were given the opportunity to say freely, without undue influence on my part as researcher, what projects they were aware of, in addition to which ones had benefitted them the most, and in which they were also involved.

The rationale for this approach was: (1) We did not want to lead the respondents by asking about the impact of specific ministries or programs within the operations of JJMC. Doing so would have been unethical, since we would have predetermined the ranking of activities of this church in terms of importance, and thereby distorted the outcome of the study. (2)

It was seen as necessary to allow respondents to evaluate the projects and activities of JJMC themselves. They pointed out which ones were impactful and which ones were not impactful. (3) It was necessary to use this approach so that the results of this study would help JJMC decide what projects to solidify, promote, and strengthen. At the same time, it would be helpful to decide which projects possibly to weed out, especially those deemed less impactful on the local community. (4) It was necessary to take this route because projects and programs run by JJMC included some which were small in size and scope. Others, such as the Youth Summer Enrichment Program are sporadic since they only run a few weeks during the summer. Therefore, rather than selecting specific programs and projects of JJMC, a decision was made to opt for a more open approach to the questions.

The survey was done using three approaches, depending on the situation of the targeted respondent. One approach was the creation of an online internet link, where identified respondents were expected to complete the questionnaire. The results uploaded automatically. The second approach was to send questionnaires as email attachments. The respondents were expected either to fill in and return the instrument online, or to print it out, complete the questionnaire, scan the results, and return it as an email attachment. They could also return the print version of the questionnaire by standard mail. The third approach involved the option of providing a hard copy of a questionnaire in person. The identified respondents were then expected to complete it by themselves or with the help of the researcher.

There were unforeseen difficulties, however, in the initial stages of administering this research instrument. Some respondents took a long time to respond. Others called to apologize for misplacing the questionnaires and asked to be sent additional copies. Others had just not seen the relevant emails and, thus, failed to follow the appropriate link to complete the survey. Others who were not so computer savvy had little idea how to access the link to the survey. Still others, upon completing the online survey, were not sure how to submit the questionnaire as completed. Thankfully, all those problems were overcome through personal contact with targeted respondents. Such contacts were made via phone calls, personal visits, and follow-up emails. The goal was to remind the respondents of the great value we attached to their responses. These responses would help to assess the work being accomplished in their neighborhood by JJMC.

We were encouraged by the fact that JJMC was a household name in the local community. Thus, the reminders were not seen as an intrusion into the privacy of identified respondents. It was necessary to be patient when receiving information from the targeted individuals. In some cases, respondents would be called and appointments arranged for a face-to-face meeting, either to help them in completing the questionnaire, or to remedy any issues in the survey that could have caused a delay. That process worked out well. Twenty-nine out of forty respondents were finally able to turn in their questionnaires. This high response rate was a remarkable achievement given the social dynamics of this neighborhood.

ASSESSMENT

This project was executed utilizing an assessment tool that had both quantitative as well as qualitative questions (see the questionnaire/instrument in Appendix 2). Responses to the quantitative questions were plotted on an Agreement (Likert) Scale. There were five options for each quantitative question that were consistently applied to all the questions. These were: "Strongly Agree" (with a value of "5"), "Somewhat Agree" (with a value of "4"), "Neutral" (with a value of "3"), "Somewhat Disagree" (with a value of "2"), and "Strongly Disagree" (with a value of "1"). A forced-response response of a scale of five choices was more preferable to seven choices, so as not to confuse respondents with too many similar options. There were six qualitative questions. They were also linked to the six project goals. Each qualitative question was associated with a separate goal.

In addition to the qualitative and quantitative questions that were directly related to the stipulated project goals, there were also general questions, which helped explain the specific quantitative questions. First was the general qualitative question labeled question 7 in the survey instrument in Appendix 2.

This question asked respondents to suggest some program or programs that JJMC was not undertaking in their neighborhood that could benefit the local community. In a sense, this question sounded similar to question 4 (linked to Goal 6) that asked respondents to list two other ways in which JJMC could improve its ministry in the local community. The latter question, labeled question 4, asked for information about what JJMC could do to improve what it was already doing. The former general qualitative question, labeled question 7, asked for suggestions on what JJMC could do in addition to what it was already doing in the neighborhood.

There were also four general quantitative questions regarding the ages of the respondents, their genders, years they had lived in or been associated with the neighborhood, and the number of years they had associated themselves with JJMC. These general quantitative questions sought demographic characteristics of the respondents, with a view to finding out who exactly were the targeted respondents. The outcome of those demographic questions is as follows:

Question on Ages of Respondents

A total of twenty-seven respondents provided answers to this question, indicating their ages when they completed the questionnaire. Two respondents, however, did not respond to this question, and provided no reason for their decision (see Table 4.1).

Table 4.1: Respondents' age

Answer choices	Number of Responses
18–25	1
26–30	0
31–35	1
36–40	1
41–45	4
46–50	3
51–55	5
56–60	4
61–65	4
66–70	0
Over 70	4

As indicated in the "Participants" section above, this survey intentionally targeted adults, defined as those of eighteen years of age and above. This was necessary in order to ensure that the information given was reliable and to avoid unforeseen and complicated legal and logistical problems. Field data shows that the ages of most of the respondents (twenty out of twenty-seven) ranged between forty-one and sixty-five. The ages were distributed as follows: ages forty-one to forty-five (four respondents); ages forty-six to fifty years (three respondents); ages fifty-one to fifty-five years (five respondents); fifty-six to sixty years (four respondents); and ages sixty-one to sixty-five years (four respondents). Only four respondents were aged over seevnty years, while those in the age ranges of eighteen to twenty-five, thirty-one to thirty-five, and thirty-six to forty had one respondent each. There were no respondents in two age categories: twenty-six to thirty, or sixty-six to seventy.

Question on Gender

Regarding the question of gender, of the twenty-nine respondents who completed the questionnaire, one of them returned the gender question unanswered, giving no explanation. As for those who answered the question, there were an equal number of males to females. That is, fourteen respondents for each gender.

Question: How many years you have lived in or associated with the South of Main neighborhood?

All twenty-nine respondents answered this question. Details of the responses are shown below (see Table 4.2). From this response, data suggests that the majority of respondents, that is twenty out of twenty-nine, had lived or associated with this neighborhood for a period of five years or fewer Data suggests, therefore, that these respondents (who possibly represented the situation of the entire neighborhood) were largely newcomers in the local community.

Table 4.2: Years of living in or association with this neighborhood.

Answer choices	Number of Responses
Less than 1 year	2
1–5	18
6–10	4
11–15	1
16–20	1
Over 20	2
Total	29

The rest of the respondents indicated they had either lived in or associated with the neighborhood for the following lengths of time: four respondents for six to ten years, one respondent for eleven to fifteen years, one respondent for sixteen to twenty years, and two respondents for over twenty years.

Question: How many years have you associated with J. Jireh Ministries Church?

Out of twenty-nine questionnaires that were returned, only one left the question unanswered. That one respondent gave no reason for not answering the question, despite having answered the other parts of the questionnaire (see Table 4.3). The majority of the respondents (twenty-six out of twenty-nine) indicated that they had associated with JJMC for a maximum of six years or fewer, as follows: less than one year (one respondent); one to two years (eleven respondents), three to four years (eight respondents), and five to six years (six respondents). Only two respondents indicated they had associated with JJMC for more than ten years; interestingly, none indicated as having such association for between seven and ten years.

Table 4.3: Years of association with J. Jireh Ministries Church

Answer choices	Number of Responses
Less than one year	1
1–2	11
3–4	8
5–6	6
7–8	0
9–10	0
Over 10	2

The data shows that most respondents have had very recent association with JJMC.

CONCLUSION

Details of the results of this study are reported in chapter 5. In that chapter, there is discussion of the results of the survey, showing the average scores from quantitative questions as well as responses from the qualitative questions. Chapter 5 draws correlations between results from quantitative questions and those from the qualitative ones. This correlation was made to draw out any convergences that may be related to the stated study goals. The ensuing analysis was done in order of prominence of goals based on the average score of each goal.

Chapter 5

Reporting the Results

THE PURPOSE OF THIS project is to discover how JJMC influences the local community for the kingdom of God. In order to address the project's purpose and goals, a number of questions were created. Twelve of these were quantitative while seven were qualitative in nature. Each of the six goals had two forced-choice survey quantitative questions that utilized an Agreement Likert Scale and one open-ended qualitative question. At the end of the survey instrument, there was one open-ended question that served as a general qualitative question aimed at eliciting from the respondents any issues and ideas that may not have been fully captured in the other six preceding qualitative questions. In addition, in order to find out what type of respondents this survey measured and, therefore, what determined the answers they gave, the survey analyzed four other quantitative-related issues: respondent's age, respondent's gender, years a respondent had lived in or associated with that neighborhood, and the number of years a respondent had associated with JJMC.

This chapter presents the results of the survey regarding the goals that were initially set out. Each goal is presented in a descending order according to the prominence of each goal as seen by the respondents' scored answers. Incidentally, Goal 1 received the highest prominence while the last, Goal 6, received the least prominence. The remaining goals were not scored in numerical order. In summary, there were a total of twenty-nine completed surveys out of a total of forty questionnaires distributed. Thus, the overall response rate was quite high. The order of goal prominence and the corresponding average score per goal was as follows: Goal 1 (4.64), Goal 5 (4.53), Goal 4 (4.50), Goal 2 (4.48), Goal 3 (3.98), and Goal 6 (3.84). A discussion of the results of the quantitative questions will come first followed by an analysis of the results from the qualitative questions. This breakdown will be followed by a discussion on overall research outcomes, finding common threads in the qualitative and quantitative questions as well as exploring any emerging issues arising from the analysis.

QUANTITATIVE ANALYSIS GOAL 1: UNDERSTANDING OF J. JIREH MINISTRIES CHURCH

As noted above, it was interesting and coincidental that Goal 1 received the highest prominence. The goal was: "To discover participants' understanding of the ministries of JJMC in their community." There were two quantitative questions on the questionnaire that addressed this goal (see Appendix 2).

These were: "I know what J. Jireh Ministries Church does in this neighborhood" (no. 1), and "J. Jireh Ministries Church does community work in this neighborhood" (no. 5). The participants used an agreement scale of one to five to respond to the assessment questions.

Table 5.1: Goal 1: Understanding of J. Jireh Ministries Church

Question	Average	Responses
5—J. Jireh Ministries Church does community work in this neighborhood	4.76	29
1—I know what J. Jireh Ministries Church does in this neighborhood	4.52	29
Composite Score	4.64	N=29

NOTE: Agreement Scale: 5=Strongly Agree; 4=Somewhat Agree; 3=Neutral; 2=Somewhat Disagree; 1=Strongly Disagree.

As indicated in Table 5.1, the average score for the two quantitative questions was 4.64, which was a high score considering the fact that the highest score possible was a 5 (see Table 5.1). Results of question 1 were as follows: one respondent "strongly disagreed," none "somewhat disagreed," one respondent was "neutral," eight "somewhat agreed," while nineteen "strongly agreed." Therefore, most of the respondents, that is twenty-seven out of twenty-nine, were aware of what J. Jireh Ministries Church was doing in their neighborhood. Regarding question 5, the results were distributed as follows: one respondent "strongly disagreed," while none "somewhat disagreed" or were "neutral." Three responded "somewhat agreed" while twenty-five responded "strongly agreed." This means that all respondents except one were in agreement that JJMC, indeed, does community work in their neighborhood.

GOAL 5: EXPERIENCING THE PRESENCE OF GOD

The goal that scored second in prominence was no. 5. It was: "To discover how participants experience the presence of God through the presence/ministry of J. Jireh Ministries Church." There were two quantitative questions in this goal (see Appendix 2) and their average score was 4.53. This average score was about half-way between "strongly agree" and "somewhat agree." The two quantitative questions scores are listed in Table 5.2 were: "J. Jireh Ministries Church has helped me to continue to deepen my spirituality" (no. 11); and "I have experienced the presence of God during my participation in J. Jireh Ministries Church program of activities" (no. 12). The participants used an agreement scale of one to five to respond to the assessment questions.

Table 5.2: Goal 5: Experiencing the Presence of God

Question	Average	Responses
12—I have experienced the presence of God during my participation in J. Jireh Ministries Church program of activities	4.59	29
11—J. Jireh Ministries Church has helped me to continue to deepen my spirituality.	4.48	29
Composite Score	4.53	N=29

NOTE: Agreement Scale: 5=Strongly Agree; 4=Somewhat Agree; 3=Neutral; 2=Somewhat Disagree; 1=Strongly Disagree.

Results of question 11 were as follows: no respondent "strongly disagreed" or "somewhat disagreed," while five were "neutral." Another five "somewhat agreed," and nineteen "strongly agreed." Thus, the majority of respondents, twenty-four out of twenty-nine, agreed that JJMC had actually helped them to deepen their spirituality. In question 12, the results were distributed as follows: no respondent "strongly disagreed," none "somewhat disagreed," four were "neutral," four "somewhat agreed," and twenty-one "strongly agreed." Again, most of the respondents, twenty-five out of twenty-nine, agreed that they had experienced the presence of God during their participation in JJMC's program of activities. The data suggests that respondents experienced the presence of God due to the presence and ministry of JJMC.

GOAL 4: COMMUNITY IMPACT

Goal 4 was: "To discover how J. Jireh Ministries Church has impacted the local community." It had an average score of 4.50, which was half-way between "strongly agree" and "somewhat agree." Its two quantitative questions (see Appendix 2) were: "I have witnessed the way J. Jireh Ministries Church has helped my community" (no. 6), and "I have learned from other people how J. Jireh Ministries Church has helped my community" (no. 7). The participants used an agreement scale of one to five to respond to the assessment questions.

Table 5.3: Goal 4: Community Impact

Question	Average	Responses
6—I have witnessed the way J. Jireh Ministries Church has helped my community	4.72	29
7—I have learned from other people how J. Jireh Ministries Church has helped my community	4.28	29
Composite Score	4.50	N=29

NOTE: Agreement Scale: 5=Strongly Agree; 4=Somewhat Agree; 3=Neutral; 2=Somewhat Disagree; 1=Strongly Disagree

For question 6, responses from respondents were as follows: no respondent said they "strongly disagreed," one "somewhat disagreed," one was "neutral," and three "somewhat agreed." The vast majority of the respondents (twenty-four) "strongly agreed" that they had witnessed the way JJMC had helped the local community. In question 7, no respondent "strongly disagreed," while only one respondent "somewhat disagreed." Six respondents were "neutral." Another six "somewhat agreed." Sixteen "strongly agreed." The results show that twenty-two respondents out of twenty-nine were in agreement that they had learned from other people how JJMC had helped the local community. Individual scores for each question are listed in Table 5.3.

GOAL 2: MOTIVATION OF INVOLVEMENT

Goal 2 was: "To discover the motivations of participants' involvement in J. Jireh Ministries Church" and had an average score of 4.48. That score lay between strongly agree and somewhat agree, but leaned more toward the latter category. Two quantitative questions (see Appendix 2) accompanying this goal were: "I am involved in J. Jireh Ministries Church because I saw the good work they do" (no. 2), and "I am involved in J. Jireh Ministries Church because I was invited into participation" (no. 3). The participants used an Agreement scale of one to five to respond to the assessment questions.

Table 5.4: Goal 2: Motivation of Involvement

Question	Average	Responses
2—I am involved in J. Jireh Ministries Church because I saw the good work they do	4.48	29
3—I am involved in J. Jireh Ministries Church because I was invited into participation.	4.48	29
Composite Score	4.48	N=29

NOTE: Agreement Scale: 5=Strongly Agree; 4=Somewhat Agree; 3=Neutral; 2=Somewhat Disagree; 1=Strongly Disagree.

Results for question 2 were as follows: one respondent "strongly disagreed," one respondent "somewhat disagreed." Three respondents were "neutral." Two respondents "somewhat agreed." Twenty-two respondents "strongly agreed." This shows that most of the respondents (twenty-four out of twenty-nine) agreed that they were involved in JJMC because they had seen the good work this organization did. In question 3, one respondent "strongly disagreed." One respondent "somewhat disagreed." Two respondents were "neutral." Four respondents "somewhat agreed." Twentyone respondents "strongly agreed." It seems therefore that most respondents (twenty-five out of twenty-nine) agreed that their involvement in JJMC was because someone invited them to participate. Individual scores for each question are listed in Table 5.4.

GOAL 3: PERSONAL IMPACT

Goal 3 was: "To discover how participants have been personally impacted by J. Jireh Ministries Church." It had an average of 3.98. This score lay between "somewhat agree" and "neutral," but leaned more toward the former, agreeing that respondents had been personally impacted by JJMC. Two quantitative questions (see Appendix 2) were: "J. Jireh Ministries Church has helped members of my family" (no. 10), and "J. Jireh Ministries Church has helped me personally" (no. 4). Individual scores for each question are listed in Table 5.5. The participants used an agreement scale of one to five to respond to the assessment questions.

Table 5.5: Goal 3: Personal Impact

Question	Average	Responses
4—J. Jireh Ministries Church has helped me personally	4.34	29
10—J. Jireh Ministries Church has helped members of my family	3.62	29
Composite Score	3.98	N=29

NOTE: Agreement Scale: 5=Strongly Agree; 4=Somewhat Agree; 3=Neutral; 2=Somewhat Disagree; 1=Strongly Disagree.

Results were distributed as follows: In question 10, three respondents "strongly disagreed." Four respondents "somewhat disagreed." Six respondents were "neutral." Four respondents "somewhat agreed." Twelve respondents "strongly agreed." Sixteen out of twenty-nine respondents agreed that JJMC had helped members of their families. That represented slightly more than half of the total respondents. The rest of the respondenses to question 10 varied. In question 4, two respondents "strongly disagreed." No respondents "somewhat disagreed." Four respondents were "neutral." Three respondents "somewhat agreed." Twenty respondents "strongly agreed."

GOAL 6: INSIGHTS ON OTHER SOCIAL ISSUES

Finally, the last goal in the order of preference was Goal 6, which read: "To discover participants' insights on important social issues in this community which need to be addressed." Its average score was 3.84 which, although the lowest, was still above average, and lay between "somewhat agree" and "neutral," and leaned more toward the former. Just like the other goals, Goal 6 had two quantitative questions posed to the respondents (see Appendix 2): "I am satisfied with the current community/social programs run by J. Jireh Ministries Church" (no. 8); and "J. Jireh Ministries Church would do better by introducing other social programs it is not currently involved in" (no. 9). Individual scores for each question are listed in Table 5.6. The participants used an agreement scale of one to five to respond to the assessment questions.

Table 5.6: Goal 6: Insights on other Social Issues

Question	Average	Responses
8—I am satisfied with the current community/social programs run by J. Jireh Ministries Church.	4.38	29
9—J. Jireh Ministries Church would do better by introducing other social programs it is not currently involved in	3.31	29
Composite Score	3.84	N=29

NOTE: Agreement Scale: 5=Strongly Agree; 4=Somewhat Agree; 3=Neutral; 2=Somewhat Disagree; 1=Strongly Disagree

Results from the respondents were as follows: for question 8, no respondent "strongly disagreed." One respondent "somewhat disagreed." Four respondents were "neutral." Seven respondents "somewhat agreed." Seventeen respondents "strongly agreed." Most of the respondents (twenty-four out of twenty-nine) agreed that they were satisfied with the current community/social programs run by JJMC in their neighborhood. In the case of question 9, one respondent "strongly disagreed." Three respondents "somewhat disagreed." Sixteen respondents were "neutral."

Four respondents "somewhat agreed." Five respondents "strongly agreed." More than half of the respondents (sixteen out of twenty-nine) were neutral (neither agreed nor disagreed) regarding a suggestion that JJMC would do better by introducing other social programs in which it was not currently involved.

COMPOSITE SCORES FOR ALL SIX GOALS

Based on the analysis of the quantitative responses of respondents, it is apparent that JJMC has a positive influence on the local community for the kingdom of God. The average score for the twelve assessment questions is 4:33 (Table 5.7), which is quite high considering that it is slightly above "somewhat agree" on the agreement rating scale, and only 0.67 shy of reaching the maximum score of "strongly agree" on the same agreement scale.

Table 5.7: Composite Scores for all Goals

Goal No.	Name	Average
1	Understanding of J. Jireh Ministries Church	4.64
2	Motivation of Involvement	4.48
3	Personal Impact	3.98
4	Community Impact	4.50
5	Experiencing the Presence of God	4.53
6	Insights on other Social Issues	3.84
	Average Composite Score	4.33

QUALITATIVE ANALYSIS

The analysis of answers and responses to qualitative questions are given here in descending order of prominence as they appeared in response to the quantitative questions. The order is as follows: Goal 1, Goal 5, Goal 4, Goal 2, Goal 3, and Goal 6. The total number of responses to each qualitative question does not necessarily add up to the number of respondents who actually answered each question. This is because, whereas some respondents gave multiple answers to a given question as required, others only gave one answer to the same question. Therefore, the analyses given here relates to the number of times or the frequency with which an issue was identified by respondents and not the number of respondents who actually identified that issue or who necessarily responded to that question. That is why, for example, responses to a particular question are more than the number of respondents who actually answered that question. Appendix 2 contains all those qualitative questions.

GOAL 1: UNDERSTANDING OF J. JIREH MINISTRIES CHURCH

The qualitative question for Goal 1 was: "List two (2) ministry programs run by J. Jireh Ministries Church in your community, explaining what each of these ministries do." There were twenty-seven responses to this question out of the twenty-nine questionnaires that were returned. Two respondents did not answer the question. No reason was given for the lack of response.

Respondents' answers to the question about listing two ministry programs run by JJMC are shown in Table 5.8, as follows:

Table 5.8: Ministry programs run by J. Jireh Ministries Church

Type of Ministry Programs	Number of Responses
Food pantry/distribution	19
Youth Summer Enrichment Program	14
Community Garden	8
General Community Outreach	6
Love Festival	5
Health Fair	4
Others	10

Food pantry and farm produce distribution scored highly as influential ministries conducted by JJMC in the community. Nineteen responses identified this program. Second came the Youth Summer Enrichment Program with fourteen responses. Third, respondents identified the community garden, with eight responses. General Community Outreach had six responses.

Outreach included not only evangelism, but also cleaning up the neighborhood. Love Festival and Health Fair contributed five and four responses, respectively. When health fairs and love festivals are combined (since these two events are held at the same time), the total score of responses was nine. Thus, food-related events and health check-up events combine to give a total of twenty-eight responses, a score that is only surpassed by the community garden program. Other programs identified by respondents were prison ministry/mentorship (two responses), Bible study/prayer meetings (two responses), ministry to ex-offenders with jobs, mentorship, etc. (two responses), clothing distribution (one response), mentorship (two responses, with one response being specifically for education mentorship at Fairwood Elementary school), and homeless veterans program.

GOAL 5: EXPERIENCING THE PRESENCE OF GOD

The qualitative question for Goal 5 was: "Explain ways in which you experience the presence of God in this ministry."

There were twenty-three responses to this question out of the twenty-nine questionnaires that were returned completed. That shows that six out of twenty-nine respondents did not answer the question. No reason was given for why the question was not answered (Table 5.9).

Table 5.9: Ways in which respondents experience the presence of God

Experience	Number of Responses
Spiritual meetings	29
Good leadership	11
Turn-up in Community events	10
Seeing real impact on the community	8
Others	2

Spiritual meetings had twenty-nine responses, and thus topped the ways in which respondents experienced the presence of God. These spiritual enhancement forums included: teaching and preaching (twelve responses), prayers (nine responses, four of which were specifically about prayers for healing), worship (seven responses), and encouragement (one response). Good leadership came second with eleven responses, ten of which mentioned specific leaders. Only one response gave "spiritual guidance" as how the presence of God was experienced.

Some respondents (ten responses) experienced the presence of God in two ways. First, was through their own participation in community events. Secondly, it was through witnessing a good attendance at community events by volunteers and people needing help. Seeing the real impact on the community (eight responses) enabled the respondents to experience the presence of God. This included seeing impact on prisoners, as well as witnessing physical needs being met, such as finding employment for those without work, providing addiction recovery services, and bringing "clean businesses" to the community. Other ways in which respondents experienced the presence of God included affirmation of their gifts and ministry calling (one response) and "taking notes and asking God 'what do I do'?" (one response.)

GOAL 4: COMMUNITY IMPACT

The qualitative question for Goal 4 was: "If J. Jireh Ministries Church has been of help to the local community, describe two (2) ways in which this has happened."

There were twenty-six responses to this question out of the twenty-nine questionnaires that were returned. Three respondents did not answer the question, with no reason given (Table 5.10).

Table 5.10: Ways in which J. Jireh Ministries Church has been of help to the local community

Ways JJMC has Helped	Number of Responses
Food	18
Community Outreach	8
Community Garden	5
Youth Summer Enrichment Program	5
Health and Medical promotion	4
Education and Youth Mentoring	4
Clothing	3
Neighborhood Clean-up	2
Repairing and providing housing for ex-offenders	2
Others	6

"Provision of food" topped the list of ways in which JJMC had been of help to the local community. It had eighteen responses. The category included such services as providing cooked foods during love festivals, as well as providing uncooked foods like fresh vegetables and fruits. Community outreach came second with eight responses, while community garden and the youth summer enrichment program each received five responses. Other ways JJMC had helped the local community were: health and medical promotion (four responses), education and youth mentoring (four responses), clothing ministry (three responses), neighborhood clean-up (two responses), and home repairs and housing of ex-offenders (two responses).

Under the category of "others," responses identified different ways through which JJMC had helped the local community, including forging unity (one response), promoting partnerships (one response), community meetings (one response), combating crime and gang activities (one response), community advocacy (one response), and fighting the selling of liquor and alcohol (one response).

GOAL 2: MOTIVATION OF INVOLVEMENT

The qualitative question for Goal 2 was: "Explain what attracted you to J. Jireh Ministries Church."

There were twenty-six responses to this question out of the twenty-nine questionnaires returned. There respondents did not answer the question. No reason was given for why the question was not answered (Table 5.11).

Table 5.11: What attracted respondents to J. Jireh Ministries Church

Type of Attraction	Number of Responses
J. Jireh Ministries Church Leadership	19
Community Spirit	8
"God sent me here"	4
Presence of God	2
Others	7

Nineteen out of forty responses identified the leaders of JJMC as what drew them to that ministry. Thus, nearly half of the total responses indicated that the leadership of JJMC has been a significant factor in both inviting and attracting people to serve in the ministries of JJMC. Here are few quotes from the respondents with regard to JJMC's leadership, particularly the pastor, that are a possible indicator of why respondents were attracted to serve: "His enthusiasm and spirituality in instilling pride back into the community"; "Willingness to help the students at school and the community"; and "The heart of the leaders that goes out to the marginalized."

Eleven out of the nineteen responses mentioned the pastor by name as why they were attracted to JJMC. The community spirit, including community work, hard work, instilling of pride in the community, and community meetings were identified in eight responses reasons for respondents to be attracted to JJMC. Four respondents indicated that it was God who sent them there, while two respondents indicated that it was the very "presence of God" that attracted them to JJMC. There was a diversity of responses under the category of "others." These included JJMC is a faith-based initiative (one response), opportunity to help mentor soon-to-be-released prisoners (one response), a place for hope and healing (one response), meeting personal needs (one response), love festival (one response), authenticity (one response), and a passion for Jesus (one response).

GOAL 3: PERSONAL IMPACT

The qualitative question for Goal 3 was: "Please discuss how J. Jireh Ministries Church has helped you and/or your family."

There were twenty-three responses to this question out of twenty-nine questionnaires returned by respondents. A total of six respondents did not answer the question. No reason was given for why the question was not answered (Table 5.12).

Table 5.12: Ways in which J. Jireh Ministries Church has helped respondents and/or their families

Type of Help	Number of Responses
Spiritual support	17
Giving opportunity to be involved in ministry	9
Practical and material assistance	5
Provided employment	3
Others	5

Spiritual support and guidance was the category most often cited as the greatest help that JJMC has been able to provide to the residents in the area of study. Seventeen responses identified spiritual support and guidance as the way in which JJMC had helped them and their families. This support came in various forms, including spiritual training and tooling, helping to increase individuals' knowledge of God, providing a support system for encouragement in the spiritual journey, helping people live according to kingdom economics, providing prayers for healing, giving emotional support, providing home worship, providing grief support, and equipping respondents to become more compassionate toward others. Nine responses also identified opportunity to be involved in ministry as a way that respondents and/or their families had been helped.

Thus, encouragement for local participation in community work is one way of helping people to identify with their community and to feel a sense of belonging and self-worth. Five responses stated that JJMC had helped in practical/material assistance, including rides to and from church, and providing financial gifts and visitations. Three responses indicated that JJMC had provided some form of employment. The remaining five responses under the category "others" identified five areas of help provided by JJMC. These included dealing with drug and alcohol problems, fostering friendship, cleaning-up the streets, and providing youth with ministry opportunities.

GOAL 6: INSIGHTS ON OTHER SOCIAL ISSUES

The qualitative question for Goal 6 was: "List other two (2) ways in which J. Jireh Ministries Church can improve its current ministry in this community."

There were twenty-three responses to this question out of twenty-nine questionnaires that were returned by the respondents. Six respondents did not answer the question. No reason was given for why the question was not answered (Table 5.13).

Table 5.13: Ways in which J. Jireh Ministries Church could improve its current ministry in the community

Improvement Ways	Number of Responses
No change/follow God's call	10
More local community and youth participation	7
More collaboration and partnerships	6
Develop a more sustainabile plan for J. Jireh	3
Improved promotion of events and activities	2
Drugs and alcohol Recovery Programs	2
Others	9

Ten responses were that JJMC should not change what it is doing. All that is required is for the church to strengthen its operations in conjunction with continuing to follow God's call in a prayerful manner. Following God's call includes "going forth" to wherever God leads. Responses pointed to the need for forging more collaboration, networking, and partnerships with other religious and non-religious organizations for purposes of ministering to the needs of the local community. Six of these responses in particular recommended reaching out to more people, such as becoming more involved in local ministry leadership activities and planning. Furthermore, five responses suggested the need to recruit more volunteers to participate in the activities of JJMC. Reaching out to a younger population was identified in two responses as a possible step in the right direction to ensure that young people would "own" the already ongoing activities run by JJMC in the community.

Three responses suggested that a sustainability strategic plan be developed "no matter the involvement of the senior pastor," is possibly a cry for inclusiveness in the administration of JJMC. That suggestion, coupled with two responses that suggested the need for improved promotion of ministries and events run by JJMC is a possible pointer to the need to invite the local community to run the events and activities currently run by the church. The result would be that the church would play a supervisory role in community development. Two responses suggest the need to introduce an alcohol and addiction recovery program. The result would be improving the presence and witness of JJMC within the community.

The remaining nine responses on how JJMC could improve its ministry in this community were very diverse. The answers included suggestions for ministries such as a food pantry, providing assistance to street walkers, and having open evangelism where recovering drug addicts could give testimonies about how they had been delivered from their habits. Other respondents suggested that local community leaders and public officials be encouraged to adopt initiatives that favor those in poverty. Other respondents suggested that JJMC should look for ways of raising more income to run its programs as well helping the local community to identify where they can get help to improve their standards of living. Some respondents suggested that JJMC should be more consistent and diversified in provision of services to the local community. While appreciating occasional clean-ups of the neighborhood organized by JJMC, some respondents suggested more of such activities, possibly monthly.

GENERAL QUALITATIVE QUESTION: "SUGGEST TWO (2) PROGRAMS J. JIREH MINISTRIES CHURCH IS NOT CURRENTLY UNDERTAKING HERE THAT COULD BENEFIT THE COMMUNITY."

There were twenty-three responses to this question out of the twenty-nine questionnaires that were returned. Six respondents did not answer the question.

No reason was given for why the question was not answered. (see Table 5.14).

Table 5.14: Programs J. Jireh Ministries Church does not currently undertake that could benefit the community

Suggested Programs	Number of Responses
Counseling services	9
Publicity and Community Follow-up	4
Enhanced Youth activities/programs	3
Partnerships/collaborations (e.g., with the local schools to provide an afterschool program) and resource-linking to community agencies	2

Help people get jobs and bringing clean businesses to the community	2
Senior citizens' services	2
Not sure/do not know	3
Others	5

Respondents to this question were not unanimous on how JJMC could improve its ministries. Answers were diverse. However, it was remarkable that nine responses suggested establishing counseling services. Five responses specifically suggested introducing premarital and marital counseling services. Three responses suggested counseling services to assist the recovery of drugs and alcohol addicts. There was one suggestion on helping emotionally disturbed members of the community. Four responses suggested that JJMC increase its visibility in the community through more effective publicity. The publicity would include community follow up so that the church's services would be better known in the community. Three responses favored more enhanced youth activities in their neighborhood. Two responses were in favor of forging partnerships and collaborations in after-school programs and resource-linking to community agencies. Two responses suggested the need to establish services for senior citizens in the community.

The category of "others" had a total of five responses: re-establish food pantry, housing for the homeless, childcare for needy working single mothers, community advocacy, and more family-oriented community outreach activities. Suggestions for the last category included such functions as community dinners, similar to what the church is already doing in its summer love feast program. Three responses suggested that respondents were either not sure or did not know what new programs to suggest for JJMC to undertake that could benefit their community.

COMMON THREADS EMERGING FROM QUANTITATIVE AND QUALITATIVE ANALYSIS

A composite average score of all the six goals comes to 4.33 (Table 5.7). From this result, it apparent that JJMC has had a significant influence on the local community for the kingdom of God. This average score is quite high, considering that it is slightly above "Somewhat Agree" on the Agreement rating scale, and only 0.67 shy of reaching the maximum score of "strongly agree" on the same agreement scale. Even when one considers the average scores for specific goals as well as the results from the qualitative questions, the conclusion suggests that JJMC has influenced the local community for the kingdom of God in different ways. When we consider the quantitative questions, even the lowest average score of Goal 6 is well above "neutral," tending toward "somewhat agreeing." Results also suggest that as much as JJMC has impacted the community of Kimball Farms, respondents in this survey, especially in the qualitative questions section, point to the need to improve, not replace, programs already serving the community.

CONCLUSION

Based on the analysis of responses to the quantitative questions, results suggest that respondents are not only aware of the programs run by JJMC (Goal 1, the highest in prominence, with a score of 4.64), but that these activities have greatly impacted both the respondents and their communities (Goal 4, the third in prominence, with a score of 4.50).

Chapter 6 will reflect upon the findings reported in this chapter. The chapter will also discuss the meaning and implications of those findings. Chapter 6 will also examine ways in which JJMC can have a greater influence on the local community through its ministry activities and outreach programs. The analysis will include sharing recommendation as well as proposing possible areas for further study. It is hoped that those recommendations will help JJMC, as well as other church groups and organizations inspired by it, to improve the church's presence and witness in society for the kingdom of God. In addition, chapter 6 will also incorporate a discussion of experiences and reflections, both personal and professional, that were encountered in the course of this discovery study project.

Chapter 6

Summary and Reflections

Results of this study indicate that JJMC has a positive impact on the community of Kimball Farms through its varied practices, programs, and activities. That is testimony to the fact that church practices not only form and sustain God's people and society, but that they also equip Christians to have an effective witness in society. The church in general is called to minister to both those inside its walls and to those on the outside. This is accomplished through established church practices similar to those conducted by JJMC.

Christian practices are unique in that they are carried out by followers of Jesus Christ in recognition that God is already at work in society. Bass and Dykstra define Christian practices as "things Christian people do together over time to address fundamental human needs in response to and in light of God's active presence for the life of the world."[1] Thus, when Christians involve themselves in a given practice, they are in essence joining in God's work. They are God's co-workers. In that sense, God is understood to be active in the world. He invites his people to make necessary adjustments in their own lives so that, through faith, they can join him in this ongoing

1. Bass and Dykstra, "Theological Understanding," 18.

work.[2] This is what JJMC has been doing by joining in God's activity in the community of Kimball Farms.

Although Christian practices may appear as mundane activities, they "can be shaped in response to God's active presence," thus suggesting "patterns of a faithful Christian way of life for our time."[3] No wonder Alan J. Roxburgh is emphatic that, in order for today's church to be relevant, there are two fundamental questions that need to be answered: (1) What is God up to in our neighborhoods and communities; and (2) how do we join with what God is doing in these places?[4] JJMC has answers to those questions, as it is already involved in practical aspects of life of the local community. Perhaps what is needed is to improve the operations.

JJMC has not been the only influence upon the local community. That is because God does not exclusively use his people in accomplishing his purposes. He has positioned other individuals, groups, and organizations, including non-Christians and non-ecclesial institutions, in order to accomplish his work. This is a challenge, therefore, for Gods' people to find out what other participants God is lining up for the sake of accomplishing his kingdom work. JJMC is doing well in that area of collaboration. However, as the study results show, there is need for JJMC to forge stronger, firmer, and wider partnerships over and above what it is currently undertaking.

It was the purpose of this project to discover how JJMC influences the local community for the kingdom of God. Based on the average scores from the quantitative questions, the order of prominence of the project goals are as follows: Goal 1, Goal 5, Goal 4, Goal 2, Goal 3, and Goal 6. Details of those results, reflections, and implications are discussed below.

GOAL 1: UNDERSTANDING OF J. JIREH MINISTRIES CHURCH

A large number of respondents knew what JJMC does in their community, since the average score was 4.52 according to Table 5.1. However, out of over fifteen programs run by JJMC (see Appendix 3), only six of those activities resonated with the respondents. This is possibly due to the fact that those six programs were the ones that had impacted the local community most, as shown in Table 5.8. Those programs were food-related programs, youth summer enrichment programs, community garden, general community outreach, love festivals, and health fairs.

2. Blackaby and King, *Experiencing God.*
3. Bass and Dykstra, "Theological Understanding," 5.
4. Roxburgh, *Missional*, 21.

Reconciliation is central to the mission of the church, which itself stems from the mission of God or the *missio Dei.* That explains why this discovery project focused on the role of the church as God's ambassador of reconciliation. This project was, therefore, a snapshot of reconciliatory activities as an example of what the church in general is called to do. JJMC is involved in a number of practices and activities aimed at reconciliation and helping local residents meet their needs. From the study results, the local community has a substantial understanding of what those activities are, since they were able to list them down. Participants' familiarity with these programs likely stemmed from how impactful these ministries were in their own lives. In a sense, those reconciliation practices are sacramental, and therefore salvific, or else they would not have the power of redemption.

GOAL 5: EXPERIENCING THE PRESENCE OF GOD

From the responses from the qualitative questions, spiritual meetings reflected the manner in which respondents experienced the presence of God. Twenty-nine responses indicated spiritual meetings had helped respondents experience the presence of God. This result was not unexpected. Involvement in community work and other "secular" activities would not be expected to have as much impact upon one's innermost being as attending, prayer meetings, Bible studies, and similar meetings focused upon spiritual enhancement. As a result, quantitative results show a high score of 4.53, making this goal second in terms of prominence.

Thus, the community of Kimball Farms has indeed experienced the presence of God through deepening their spirituality and participation in programs and activities run by JJMC. Additionally, from the results of the qualitative questions, the leadership of JJMC has moved the local community into experiencing the presence of God. "Good leadership" was identified by 11 responses as a factor in helping respondents to experience the presence of God (see Table 5.9). It is even more remarkable that all eleven of those responses actually mentioned leaders by names, thus indicating the high premium the local community has placed on the role of JJMC's leadership in guiding them in spiritual renewal and experiencing God at work in their lives.

Respondents in the survey indicated that the presence of God had been felt in the local community, which is a good thing. There is tangible evidence of the local community being so impacted by what JJMC does in their neighborhood that the result of this experience is a sense of the presence of God. That being the case, however, JJMC cannot be complacent about these positive findings. There is need to recognize the dangers of reducing justice concerns to mere programs, for otherwise the primary result is only that Christians raise their own self esteem rather than meeting actual needs. Thus, JJMC and the church in general ought to go beyond what David E. Fitch and Geoff Holsclaw refer to as "T-shirt logo" or "bumper sticker" activism, reducing justice to yet another church program.[5]

Therefore, the authentic and sustainable presence of God through real action is needed. This is because, as disciples of Jesus Christ, we are the conscience of society and ambassadors of God's kingdom on the earth. When we withdraw from that role, the authentic presence of God is not experienced in the society. As a result, we will have failed in being ambassadors of reconciliation in God's mission. Care must, therefore, be taken to ensure that the church remains the signpost of the kingdom of God by intentionally helping the world to "see" and experience the kingdom.

GOAL 4: COMMUNITY IMPACT

Respondents have been impacted by the activities of JJMC, since this goal received an average score of 4.50. From the qualitative results, this impact is even more evident since six key programs are mentioned by respondents as having helped the community of Kimball Farms. These programs were food, community outreach, community garden, youth summer enrichment, health promotion, education, and youth mentoring. From qualitative questions, one respondent wrote the following regarding ways JJMC had helped meet community needs: "Giving new life to neighbors who are participating in J. Jireh Ministries." That was remarkable.

JJMC is doing what Christians are called to do, that is, addressing the deep-seated needs that cannot be met through other non-theistic social justice programs. Meeting those needs creates impact at the local level, including creating a a godly atmosphere that further sensitizes Christians about meeting local needs. Thus, as Larry Rasmussen indicates, Christians are called to build an alternative community.[6] Such is the alternative community being created by JJMC. Similarly, this idea of an impactful alternative community outside of the dominant culture is shared by Walter Brueggemann. Although Brueggemann is cautious about fully embracing such a utopian community, he is, nevertheless, hopeful that a community that is inclusive of the poor, the hungry, and the grieving is possibly "the wave of God's future."[7]

5. Fitch and Holsclaw, *Prodigal Christianity*, loc. 4091.
6. Rasmussen, "Shaping Communities," 127.
7. Brueggemann, *Prophetic Imagination*, 118.

JJMC is creating such a community by initiating transformational change through deliberate social and spiritual interventions. The outcome of this dissertation project suggests that JJMC is very intentional about reaching out to address the needs of the local community. This involves going beyond what is conventionally defined as spiritual needs by adopting a more holistic approach that addresses wider social-justice concerns at the community of Kimball Farms.

GOAL 2: MOTIVATION OF INVOLVEMENT

According to the results of the quantitative questions, the high average score of 4.48 indicates that respondents were leaning towards "somewhat agreeing" that their motivation for participating in JJMC was doing because they had both seen "the good work" it accomplished and they had also been "invited" into participation in that labor. It is remarkable that the leadership of JJMC has done so much to welcome new participants into the ongoing community work. Thus, a high premium on social capital exists in this neighborhood. This is likely to be something that possibly can be banked on for future community work in this neighborhood. In addition, since some respondents said that it was God who sent them to the church, and that it was the very "presence of God" that attracted them to JJMC, it appears that respondents were aware of the working of God in their neighborhood. They were, therefore, interested in joining God in what he was already doing among them, just like Henry T. Blackaby and Claude V. King would argue.[8]

The apparent strong motivation of individuals' involvement in JJMC is something about which to be proud. However, there is an apparent disunity on the part of clergy serving this community as evidenced by the attitude portrayed during the time of doing this research. For example, on numerous occasions, few clergy responded to the invitation to attend monthly civic association meetings convened at the offices of JJMC. Personal or ecclesial-related problems aside, the clergy in this area seem not to be highly motivated to work as a team towards addressing the needs of the local community. Possibly, a focus on church growth of individual congregations contributes to this issue. Church leaders ought to be united to ensure that the light of Christ burns brightly in this neighborhood.

8. Blackaby and King, *Experiencing God*.

GOAL 3: PERSONAL IMPACT

The results from the quantitative questions yielded an average score of 3.98. It appears that the community of Kimball Farms has been greatly impacted by the activities of JJMC, both at individual as well as at the family levels. This finding corresponds with the results of the qualitative questions whose results found twenty-six responses that identified spiritual support and provision of opportunity for involvement in ministry as two key ways in which local residents had been helped by JJMC. That finding is significant in that it informs why the local community would be readily available to be part of what JJMC does in their area. The community benefits from what the programs offer, or else it would not become part of the activities of this church. That may also mean that local people are likely to be ambassadors for spreading the news about the good that goes on in their neighborhood. This may attract more supporters.

As was indicated in chapter 1, the challenge that JJMC faces is how to maintain an effective local witness in ministering to the material needs while also not neglecting the spiritual concerns. JJMC must enhance its approach to doing holistic ministry by going beyond mere provision of handouts. It must also enable needy local residents to acquire life skills that would lead to self-sufficiency and independence. That way, it will be possible to link material needs with spiritual connectedness. That is a more sustainable and holistic approach to ministry.

The results of this study have shown the presence of goodwill among local residents. It is possible, therefore, for JJMC to ride on this "goodwill ticket" to enhance its local presence. This will, in the long run, ensure that its activities are showcase examples of incarnational ministry in poor, under-sourced, and disadvantaged urban neighborhoods.

GOAL 6: INSIGHTS ON OTHER SOCIAL ISSUES

The average score of the quantitative questions in Goal 6 was the lowest of the measured goals. However, a score of 3.84 was still significant in that it leaned more towards "somewhat agreeing." In other words, to some extent, some local residents are satisfied with the current activities run by JJMC. Others would likely be encouraged by the introduction of new social programs. This finding comes close to what the qualitative questions discovered. Twenty-nine responses showed that the local community would be appreciative if JJMC would initiate new programs in addition to those already conducted. Only ten responses wished to maintain the *status quo*.

This result does not mean that local residents are dissatisfied with JJMC's ministries within the community. In my opinion, what the residents are yearning for is an improvement in the activities and services that JJMC is carrying out in their neighborhood. In fact, this finding is in line with the results from the general qualitative question labeled question 7 (see Appendix 2). This qualitative question sought new programs that respondents wanted to see JJMC introduce that could benefit their community. An overwhelming majority of responses, a total of twenty-seven, suggested new programs. Key among these recommendations was the introduction of some form of counseling service. This suggestion reflects the kinds of issues that the local community faces, including drug and alcohol abuse, which were mentioned by several respondents. Thus, by implication, there is need to introduce counseling- and rehabilitation-related services that would help deal with those issues.

The results of this study show great Christian enthusiasm for involvement in social activism. This is evidenced by recommendations that respondents gave on what could be done to enhance the ongoing work of JJMC. However, social activism without spiritual formation is futile. JJMC, in conjunction with other churches, should consider offering a course on spiritual formation and social activism. This program would provide Christians a solid spiritual foundation in their quest for social justice. Such an approach to social activism is important because morality and spirituality are intertwined. As Richard M. Gula puts it: "Spirituality without morality is disembodied; morality without spirituality is rootless."[9] That reminds me of a children's song I used to hear children sing in my neighborhood in Kenya, that "*bread without margarine is like a train without an engine.*" Thus, just like bread without margarine is tasteless, so social activism without spiritual formation is doomed to fail, despite any good intentions.

REFLECTIVE OVERVIEW

In summary, in light of the results of Goals 1 and 4 on "Understanding of J. Jireh Ministries Church" and "Community Impact," respectively, responses from the field suggest that most of the respondents may have been impacted more by programs that addressed their felt need, mainly food (see Table 5.8). That is why nineteen responses identified food pantry and food distribution activities as programs run by JJMC. What this suggests is that there is possibly need to continue engaging in activities with the most impact on the community. This is because, as much as people might have other needs,

9. Gula, *Call to Holiness*, 5.

the fact that the majority of the respondents identified food distribution as a major activity indicates their lives have been impacted more through this program than through any other. This points to the need for reducing the number of programs to a handful that are most effective.

However, I can also see a dilemma. Most of the programs are donor-driven, which means that JJMC runs programs that a willing donor funds. Such an approach tends to foster dependency on donors, the very "disease" that has plagued the poor, making them to be mere pawns in the hands of parties with vested interests. In the process, well-meaning agencies like churches become instruments and tools for perpetuating this syndrome.

APPLICATION

The outcomes of this research project and the lessons learned will hopefully help to promote the need for the streamlining of governance structures of ministry-related social justice activities. That is why Larry Rasmussen emphasizes the importance of the role of leadership and governance in terms of ordering, caring for, and leading communities in the context of the church.[10] Moreover, Rasmussen adds that "coordinating a community's practices through good governance helps to make its way of life clear, visible, and viable."[11] Thus, shaping the Community of Kimball Farms is of utmost importance to promote social justice within the community.

Since there are Christians living in this neighborhood, whether they are associated with JJMC or not, there is need to deal with the wrong perception that Christianity is a mere self-indulgent pietism that lacks essential community-building tenets. In this regard, Charles Marsh shares the conviction of John M. Perkins, the founder of Christian Community Development Association. Pointing to the church's ministry to the poor, the oppressed, the weak, and the helpless in society, Perkin's view is that it is necessary to have the right perspective of the role of the church in society. This would call for Christians to re-evaluate their "personal desires, prejudices, opinions, and economic policies in the light of God's moral demands."[12] Doing so would be a clear demonstration of a clear and unwavering commitment of the church to social justice concerns. This, in Charles Marsh's view, would include an intentional "public advocacy for economic policies preferential to the poor

10. Rasmussen, "Shaping Communities," 120.

11. Rasmussen, "Shaping Communities," 121.

12. Marsh, *Welcoming Justice*, 106.

and oppressed," something that Christians should actually practice in addition to verbal proclamation of kingdom *ethos*.[13]

The results of this study will hopefully ignite a passion for the church to be ready to engage in righting situations of injustice in society. In addition, it is hoped that the results of this research project will both empower and encourage Christians to play their rightful prophetic role of addressing social injustices. Doing so would be the right thing to do because, as Nicholas Wolterstorff argues, it provides valuable lessons on how disciples of Jesus can advocate for social change and restoration of human dignity.[14] In light of a general optimism regarding what the church can accomplish in situations of injustice, the results of this study will hopefully encourage local residents to maintain efforts in addressing the social problems afflicting the community of Kimball Farms. It is further hoped that this study will inspire outsiders to come and be part of the community-building efforts as happened in similar neighborhoods in the American South. In the past, poverty had caused the flight of young people from poor neighborhoods in the American South such that, even after getting an excellent education, none of them wanted to return to their communities. However, an effort to woo such people to return and help their community has been one of the clarion calls of John Perkins and his Christian Community Development Association movement. He was convinced that in order to make a difference in black communities, poor young people needed to not only be helped to get an education but to also be encouraged to "come back home" to assist in community-building.[15]

Christians ought to remember that social justice is one area of the ministry of reconciliation to which the church is called. It is part of heralding and living out the good news of the kingdom of God. Since the intent of this study was to discover how JJMC influences the local community for the kingdom of God, the choice of ongoing Christian ministry projects and programs was to provide test-case examples on how to promote reconciliation in an economically depressed neighborhood in Columbus, Ohio. Reconciliation suggests two things. First is the pre-existence of conflict or, at least, the presence of some disconnection or breach. Second, it is necessary to amend this breach.

Thus, in order for the church to be effective in this ministry of reconciliation, it is imperative to understand the nature of situations that require reconciliation, as well as comprehending how reconciliation works. In this

13. Marsh, *Welcoming Justice*, 106.

14. Wolterstorff, *Journey toward Justice*, 166–79.

15. Perkins, "Cultural Captivity of the Church," 36.

regard, there are five broad areas of reconciliation to which the church has been called to participate in as the *missio Dei* and, by extension, the mission of Jesus Christ (see again the comments on 2 Cor 5:16–21 and Luke 4:16–30 in chapter 2 above). Those five areas of reconciliation are discussed below:

1. Reconciliation of humans to fellow humans: e.g., dealing with crime, violence, race-relations, and economic disparities.
2. Reconciliation of humans with (in) themselves; that is, ministry to one's wholeness in body, soul, spirit, and mind: e.g., health and wellness, food and nutrition, unemployment and loss of human dignity.
3. Reconciliation of humans with their environment, land, and the created order. This may include environmental stewardship and practices of bringing harmony in the created order: e.g., planting trees, preventing environmental pollution, organic farming, permaculture, and urban farming.
4. Reconciling humans with the loving God from whom they have been alienated. It takes a changed person to bring about change in others and the created order. Only reconciled people can be effective ambassadors in the ministry of reconciliation. In his infinite wisdom, God chooses mere mortals to carry out this ministry of reconciliation through the enabling power of his Holy Spirit.
5. Reconciliation of human and non-human systems and structures governing the interconnectedness of the above four aspects of reconciliation. It is when reconciliation is realized that the four components will function harmoniously as originally designed by the Creator. This reconciliation may also include dealing with such natural phenomena as cycles, seasons, winds, earthquakes, and systems that may or may not have a direct link with human activities. Thus, when these systems go wild due to, say, the repercussions of human sin and the Fall, there is ensuing suffering by humans and non-humans alike. These systems, therefore, need to be re-ordered and reconciled with God to their pre-Fall status as originally intended. The church is called to be the ambassador of this this reconciliation so that all aspects of the created order can be redeemed.

The first four areas are akin to Francis Schaefer's view of what constitutes the mission of the church in bringing healing to the brokenness resulting from the Fall.[16] They are also what Howard A. Snyder and Daniel V.

16. Schaeffer, *Pollution and the Death of Man*, 66–68.

Runyon refer to as the sociocultural, psychological, ecological alienations, and spiritual dimensions of alienation inflicting the whole human family. They are in need of healing.[17] As God's appointed ambassador for bringing this reconciliation (2 Cor 5:18–21), the church shapes communities and brings social transformation through announcing and living out the ideals of the kingdom of God. Thus, as orthopraxis accompanies orthodoxy, society not only "hears" the gospel but it is also transformed through "seeing" this gospel lived out in real life by God's people. That now becomes a demonstration of how communities might be shaped by believers. This is the idea behind building the beloved community, first identified with Martin Luther King Jr., and later advanced by other civil rights activists who embraced King's philosophy of social justice. Obviously, as Charles Marsh would remind us, Jesus was, and still is, at the center of this new beloved community.[18] This is what building a beloved community is all about, not just in the community of Kimball Farms where JJMC is located, but in all communities where God's people live and where their tendrils of influence extend. It is God's people doing God's work his way, or else building community and shaping it will not be any different from similar efforts by non-Christians whose philosophy is based on secular humanism. Building a beloved community is therefore both theistic and, most importantly, Christocentric.

RECOMMENDATIONS

In light of these discoveries from this project, I offer the following recommendations. Over and above the monthly Civic Association meetings at the community of Kimball Farms, I recommend there should be frequent Town Hall meetings spearheaded by a more broad-based faith community. Since the church in general is the agency of change that God has appointed as the ambassadors of his kingdom, it is important for churches in the study area to collaborate in the local civic affairs. Care must be taken, however, to ensure that such action is not informed by the conventional need to "evangelize" in the sense of winning church members. Rather, the driving force should be to act as the light and salt of the community (Matt 5:13–14) and societal leaven (Matt 13:33). In light of the results of this study, it appears that JJMC has been doing a good job, so far. However, it is recommended that there be a thorough evaluation of the ongoing programs of activities with a view to concentrating on specific programs that will have greater

17. Snyder and Runyon, *Decoding the Church*, 160.

18. Marsh, *Welcoming Justice*, 102.

community impact. Programs should be restricted to those most beneficial to the community. In addition, this study has discovered that JJMC has played a significant role in being a true signpost of the kingdom of God. However, study results show that some programs and activities were more impactful than others.

It is, therefore, recommended that there be intentional "project thinning." That way, there will be strengthening of JJMC's witness instead of spreading its presence too thinly in this neighborhood.

It is also recommended that there be intentionality in connecting certain programs with specific organizations, both ecclesial and non-ecclesial. These specially selected organizations would be those identified as having the capacity of being the most effective change agents. This is one of the observations made by respondents who recommended that JJMC create more partnerships that will help to improve service delivery (see Tables 5.13 and 5.14). That means even widening the scope of influence to cover policy issues that have impact on the lives of local people. JJMC should explore other areas of ministry in addition to ongoing programs.

JJMC has a bright future. It can adopt faith-rooted organizing principles as well as utilize locally available resources, including local social capital. John Horvat II defines social capital resource as "any social network that is governed by shared norms and values and is maintained by sanctions, and that creates conditions for trust, thereby enriching social, civic, and economic life."[19] The results of this study indicate existence of immense social capital resources and goodwill among residents of this neighborhood. Trust has been built among local residents and this can be taken as a providential launching pad for JJMC to do more work to improve the lives of local residents.

In that regard, there might be need to adopt what is now popularly referred to as an Asset-Based Community Development (ABCD) approach in identifying local human and non-human resources in this community that could be harnessed for purposes of addressing existing needs. Doing ABCD with clear intentionality on mobilizing local resources before looking for assistance externally can be the first step towards addressing the plight of the marginalized people of the community of Kimball Farms.

The JJMC needs to be commended for being an advocate for the local community through, among other vehicles, the Community of Kimball Farms Civic Association. This association, however, is in dire need of internal reorganization so it can be more inclusive and proactive in addressing the plight of its members. For example, it would be prudent to see JJMC

19. Horvat, *Return to Order*, loc. 5311.

loosen its tight grip on the association. Instead, the association should incorporate into its leadership individuals who are outside the church but are members of community. In addition, the church-run J. Jireh Development Corporation (JJDC) needs to be more outward looking and be more transparent in its dealings with the community so it can have more local support from the people it is meant to serve. If possible, this organization needs to urgently delinke itself from the top leadership of JJMC, including changing its name to reflect that change.

AREAS FOR FURTHER STUDY AND WHAT REMAINS UNDONE

From the results of this study, JJMC is active in the lives of people in the local community. As indicated above, its practices have gone a long way in addressing "fundamental human needs."[20] In that sense, these practices and activities are sacramental in that they are "vehicles" through which God's kingdom is experienced in the local community. Through these practices, JJMC has brought positive influence, and therefore salvation, by adopting holistic approaches to addressing local felt needs. Yet, within a larger church context, an area that might require further study is an examination of the sacramental life of the church, especially among Protestants and evangelicals. Some churches oppose the idea of sacramental church practices and rites as means of dispensing grace for salvation.[21] Thus, for such churches, sacraments are not salvific. No wonder churches in this tradition prefer the term "ordinances" in place of sacraments. Even then, ordinances refer to baptism and Eucharist. It would be helpful to find out what congregants "gain" from such practices and to what extent these practices are inherently salvific, regardless of whether or not those participating in them perceive them as such. Within that context, it might be good to discover what role the church plays in addressing social justice issues and the extent to which such practices are sacramental. It would also be fitting to find out how church's involvement in social justice constitutes sacramentality in terms of either "earning" salvation or helping to reflect salvation for those involved. On the whole, therefore, a lack of unity in the church in the work of justice calls for further study on how justice can be seen as a sacramental offering.

The church has two dimensions: church as an organism and church as an institution. It would be good to find out (1) which of the two is more involved in promotion of social justice in society, and (2) what is the role

20. Bass and Dykstra, "Theological Understanding," 18.

21. Erickson, *Christian Theology*, 1018.

of each one of these as far as justice and active engagement in the kingdom of God is concerned. Another area for further study is the workings of the kingdom of God among people outside the influence of Christianity, both in the past and in the present. There are those people and institutions that influence God's creation positively by improving the cosmos and addressing social justice issues. Yet, as they do so, they may be completely oblivious of the workings and intentions of the Creator God in the ongoing and final reconciliation of all things. In a sense, therefore, these are co-workers who are unaware of their partnership with God in the drama of renewal of creation. The big question is: How would the tenets God's kingdom apply in the case of such people and institutions whose activities are clearly constructive as they address the same issues that the church is called to address? Are those efforts to be appreciated and understood within their own contexts or within the context of the kingdom of God? Is there need, therefore, to reorient those efforts towards a more theistic and Christocentric perspective?

As much as the church is to be understood as a "signpost" of the kingdom of God, further study needs to be done to bring clarity and specificity as to how the church is to operate as such. Should the church morph, integrate, or work alongside the secular kingdom(s) of this world? What should be the relationship between the kingdom of God advanced by the church and non-theistic social, political, and economic institutions the church finds itself interacting with every day? If partnership is the answer to such co-existence, how is such collaboration supposed to work while ensuring that the church remains faithful to its call to be the signpost and a true agent of the kingdom of God?

PERSONAL GOALS

Throughout my Christian life, going way back long before I even contemplated going to seminary, I have always been interested in understanding what the church is and what its role is in society. Related to that was my interest in discovering the corporate as well as individual Christian contribution toward the realization of the broader goal of the church and the ultimate purpose God has set for his creation. That preoccupation is what led me to doing a research project on the role of the church in influencing local communities for the kingdom of God.

That background helps to put into focus the reasons that propelled me to coming up with the following four personal goals. Thankfully, those goals have been met in the course of doing this project:

Personal Goal 1: Education about my Role

This goal has been met as I can now see through the results of this project that I need to be a change agent and an ambassador of reconciliation both in and outside the church. My role is to awaken the sleeping giants in the church to be able to carry out the work of reconciliation to which God has called his people. There are many people in the church who are happy that they have a relationship with God, but are not aware of their role in the church. My responsibility is therefore to remind these people not to "sleep" on the job but to arise and be the reconcilers God intended them to be.

Personal Goal 2: Learning from Others

The community of Kimball Farms and the leadership of JJMC have taught me a great lesson that no one is "the least" insofar as the kingdom of God is concerned. Each one of us has a very important role to play in the work of reconciliation, however insignificant that contribution might appear.

This project gave me an opportunity to learn about the intersection of theology and practice in community transformation. This study has taught me how faith and social justice integrate in Christian ministry, without putting artificial demarcation between the two.

Personal Goal 3: Equipped to Equip Others

From this project, I have learned valuable lessons on how kingdom work can be accomplished through the vehicle of social justice. The work of JJMC in the community of Kimball Farms and the experience I received while doing this project have equipped me with tools that I can use to do similar work elsewhere. I have taken much away, both what to do and what not to do in kingdom-related community development projects.

Personal Goal 4: Launching a Kingdom-Oriented Christian Ministry

The lessons learned from this project and the experiences gained have prepared me to encourage and mobilize God's people to be effective ambassadors of reconciliation. The study has also prepared me to identify areas of ministry that can benefit from lessons I have learned in doing this dissertation project. This project was an eye-opener on the relationship between evangelism, activism, and community development. My skills have also been enhanced on how to ensure that the proclamation of the gospel is accompanied by works of service. This will enable God's imagers to flourish even as they actively engage in reconciliation work. I am, therefore, well-prepared to make a positive contribution in integrating faith and practice, especially regarding social-justice concerns.

CONCLUDING THOUGHTS

Baptism is a key to Christian identity. According to Robin Jensen, baptism is important in several ways. Among these is the fact that it is a public confession that we are no longer "earthy" but "heavenly." It is a resistance to "worldliness." It is death to the old way of life and birth of a new life.[22] Becoming a Christian is also seen as a vow to rest and a vow to resist three things: the empire, the idol of work, and "the restless productivity of the commercial culture."[23] Becoming a Christian, therefore, is decidedly following Jesus Christ through self-denial and seeking to do his mission. This mission is what Jesus pronounced in Luke 4:18–19 and to which we are his ambassadors for reconciling the entire creation to God (2 Cor 5:19). That is what constitutes promoting social justice and bringing to bear God's kingdom, even as we await the future grand finale of the inauguration of the fullness of that kingdom. This reconciling work is precisely what the church is called to accomplish. JJMC is a living example of how this should be done. It may not be a perfect example as it is work in progress. Nevertheless, it is it is certainly a pointer in the right direction.

Here lies the challenge. The church cannot continue with business as usual if it has no real impact in the society. The church is supposed to be the signpost of the kingdom, the ambassador of reconciliation in the kingdom of God. The church should not just be seen but should also be heard as it actively and proactively engages with society. There is no shortcut to fulfilling that mandate.

The work of social justice, the kingdom of God, and reconciliation are essentially tasks that have, of necessity, to be accomplished both theistically and Christocentrically. It is what Jesus Christ was up to when he stood and spoke in the synagogue (Luke 4:16–21). It is a responsibility that has now been handed to Jesus Christ's disciples, a task now called "the ministry of reconciliation" (2 Cor 5:18, NRSV). The church is expected to continue with the work of justice in its liturgy—that is, public service—as

22. Jensen, "Baptismal Rights and Architecture," 117–44.

23. Block, *Other Kingdom*, 51.

well as in all its sacramental and other ecclesial practices. Doing so will be a proclamation of the death and resurrection of Jesus Christ and thus announcing the triumph of good over evil. That is what "gospelling" is about. All sacraments are public manifestations and, by implication, proclamations of the gospel.

Manifesting the kingdom of God is going beyond showing that God is in control of his creation. As the creator and sustainer of creation, God is sovereign over all things. However, the kingdom of God is not only theistic but also Christocentric. It is this kingdom, inaugurated by Jesus Christ, that God will finally restore in the fullness of new creation. That will be in the era of the new heavens and new earth.

Involvement of the church in social justice as part of kingdom work is non-negotiable. It is part of *missio Dei* in which the church is expected to engage so that humanity can reflect God's image, the *imago Dei.* That way, humanity will be equipped to minster to the rest of creation for reconciliation and also be freed fully to worship God. This echoes the words Augustine of Hippo (354–430 CE) who, in *The Confessions,* said this about God:

> Man, being a part of Thy creation, desires to praise Thee, man, who bears about with him his mortality, the witness of his sin, even the witness that Thou "resistest the proud," . . . yet man, this part of Thy creation, desires to praise Thee. Thou movest us to delight in praising Thee; for Thou hast formed us for Thyself, and our hearts are restless till they find rest in Thee.[24]

Indeed, humans can only find rest in God when they are reconciled to him. It is then that they are free to be engaged in reconciling the rest of creation to God. This is the ministry of reconciliation that the church has been given: to bring about the kingdom of God. The church, therefore, stands at a pivotal point in history to carry out this divine task by partnering with the Creator to whom all creation will finally be fully reconciled. It is then, in that fully achieved reconciliation, that God's *shalom* will be finally realized. In the meantime, our prayer remains:

> Your kingdom come,
> Your will be done,
> on earth as it is in heaven. (Matt 6:10, NRSV)

24. Augustine, *Confessions* 1.1.1.

Appendix 1

Research Proposal

Ashland Theological Seminary
The Kingdom of God in an Urban Neighborhood Congregation in Columbus, Ohio: A Proposal Submitted to the Faculty of Ashland Theological Seminary
In Candidacy for the Degree of Doctor of Ministry
By Abraham Ndungu
Ashland, Ohio
July 30, 2015

PURPOSE STATEMENT

The purpose of this project is to discover how J. Jireh Ministries Church of Columbus, Ohio influences the local community for the kingdom of God. The overall research question is: How has J. Jireh Ministries Church of Columbus, Ohio influenced the local community for the kingdom of God?

OVERVIEW

The idea of the kingdom of God which is about partnership between the creator God and humans in stewarding creation is found explicitly and implicitly throughout the biblical narrative. The task of stewardship was given before the Fall for humans to take care of the "very good" condition of creation (Genesis 1:31). This pristine pre-fall creation was however marred by sin (Genesis 3), a situation that subsequently called for need for restoration and reconciliation, the full realization of which will come in the future (Revelation 20, 21). That is what the kingdom of God is all about.

The Church is now a "signpost" of God's Kingdom, providing ambassadors for proclaiming and bringing to bear the new creation that God has purposed with the death and resurrection of His Son. This newness or renewal of all things (2 Corinthians 5:16–21) constitutes the Kingdom of God, and that is expected through the agency of God's people. The theme of the Kingdom of God is therefore both a continuation and a part of the grand biblical narrative about God and His people.

This research project is based on the premise that God is and has always been at work in the world. The challenge, therefore, is whether humans can identify where God is at work so they can join Him in what he is already doing. It is therefore a privilege for mere mortals to join their creator in the work of the kingdom. God's people, the church, have to cooperate with God and be His coworkers in advancing his kingdom. Although the kingdom of God is not, and can never be a product of human effort, it is incumbent upon humans to cooperate with God in order to realize this kingdom so that God can work within human community through Christ.[1] What J. Jireh Ministries Church (JJMC) is doing is an example of how God's people can be involved in God's mission and this project seeks to discover the extent to which this congregation is living out this mission in Columbus, OH and how that is indicative of the presence of God in that community. That is why Erickson notes that the kingdom of God is neither externally imposed nor far removed but something present, to which human beings can enter "wherever obedience to God is found," and one which Christians are expected to spread.[2]

FOUNDATIONS

I have been involved in various leadership roles both within and outside the church for some time now and this has enabled me to understand the importance of promoting human flourishing through the use of use God-given gifts for the common good. My desire is for Christians to live out their faith and become the light of the world and the salt of the earth (Mt. 5:13–16) and I look forward to helping fellow Christians realize this position through the findings of this study. The overarching theme of the scripture is about God and His efforts to reconcile His creation with himself, and how His people are called to join Him in this endeavor. And from a theological point of

1. Niebuhr, *Christ and Culture*, 98.
2. Erickson, *Christian Theology*, 1163.

view, since reconciliation with God's creation is God's mission, God's people are therefore expected to carry out this task for and on behalf of God. The church has been involved in this task over the centuries and there are valuable lessons that can be drawn on how this task has been carried out. J. Jireh Ministries Church is as a test case of such endeavors.

Personal Foundation

Studying the dynamics of the Kingdom of God will equip me to be an ardent promoter of stewardship and social justice education which is an area of great need in our world today. With so many injustices around us, Christians need to speak out for the oppressed and help to put in place systems for promoting social justice and human dignity. This is what I would like to see taking place, and the results of this dissertation research project will doubtless make a significant contribution in that regard.

My involvement in Christian missions over the years has heightened my desire to for church leaders to catch this same vision. The choice of this project has been propelled by my desire to not only know what the kingdom of God is and the role of the church in it but also to use the research findings to equip church leaders so they can better serve the church in fulfilling its calling. Above all else, the Great Commission is not just about calling people to Jesus Christ for forgiveness of sins but also about a holistic transformation of individuals, communities and societies. My desire is therefore to promote this perspective following completion of this dissertation project.

Biblical Foundation

Although the two passages chosen for this study don't explicitly discuss the kingdom of God, the subject is nevertheless implied. 2 Corinthians 5:16–21 is about the mission of the church as a "kingdom community," who the agents of the kingdom are and what is expected of them. Luke 4:16–30 is about Jesus' proclamation of the messianic kingdom and what is the kingdom of God. In 2 Corinthians 5:16–21, three key terms stand out: Church (implied by "given us" and "reconciled us" in verse 18), reconcile (what Christ has done, yet it is not fully realized); and reconciliation (what the Church is called to do). As participants in matters of the kingdom of God, it is the duty of Christians to be actively involved in returning creation to its original pristine pre-Fall status, as much as full restoration will only be realized in the future in the fullness of the kingdom of God. In the meantime, as agents of the kingdom, Christians are expected to do evangelism so there can be partial restoration of the kingdom.

As God's co-workers in bringing to bear the new creation that God has purposed with the death and resurrection of His Son, followers of Jesus are not only new creation but to also God's ambassadors for the new creation intended by God—the newness or renewal of all things discussed in 2 Corinthians 5:1621). Despite a lack of clarity on what Paul meant with "new creation" in 2 Corinthians 5:17, whether this "newness" relates to an individual convert, or community of faith or general cosmos, it is generally agreed that a "convert, as part of a community of faith, enters the cosmic drama of recreation that God inaugurated at the resurrection of Jesus Christ and will bring to completion at the Parousia."[3] And it is upon entry into this "newness" that makes the new "recruits" to become active participants in this ongoing recreation drama, thus qualifying them as "ambassadors" of bringing about reconciliation. This is what Paul refers to as "ministry of reconciliation," with the word ministry or *diakonia* suggesting active engagement in service on the part of those involved.

Luke 4:16–30 comes at the inauguration of the public ministry of Jesus Christ where there is a sort of self-annunciation of what His ministry and the mission of the kingdom was all about. That announcement was both appalling and surprising to the hearers, triggering controversy that was to linger on even beyond His earthly life and ministry. Although this passage presents Jesus like it was the beginning of His public ministry, Jesus might have already been in public ministry mainly in Judea for about a year according to John's Gospel, and more lately in the synagogues in Galilee according to Luke 4:14–15.[4]

Moreover, Luke may have taken this episode from a later point in Mark's Gospel (Mark 6:1–6) and placed it first so he can introduce key themes of Jesus' ministry such as his coming rejection by his own people, a prediction of his suffering fate and the mission to the Gentiles in Acts.[5] It is in this passage where Jesus publicly announces who He was and what He was up to—that He was the one coming to fulfill the messianic expectation and thereby inaugurate the awaited kingdom of God. This pronouncement took people by surprise, triggering a series of unending controversy and mixed reaction among people throughout Jesus' earthly ministry. Thus, some people were amazed and spoke "well of him" (v.22) while others were so "furious" that they "drove him out of the town" and even attempted to

3. Levison, "Creation and New Creation," 190.

4. Jeffrey, *Luke*, 69.

5. Arnold, *Bible Backgrounds*, 361.

kill him by throwing him off the cliff (vv. 2829). Whereas at first the townspeople welcomed their "hometown boy," they later turned against him because they were enraged by his claim that in the past God had sometimes chosen to favor Gentiles over his people Israel, an allegation that was taken as heretical.[6] This incidence marked the beginning of the Great Galilean ministry in Luke 4:14–9:50 during which Jesus "proclaims the message of the kingdom of God, calls disciples and performs miracles demonstrating his kingdom authority."[7]

Apparently, Jesus intentionally selected His readings so He could purposefully read passages that confirmed who He was and what He had come to accomplish—that he was indeed the promised Messiah and that he had come to inaugurate the long-awaited kingdom. The passage Jesus chose was apparently Isaiah 61:1–2 with phrases from 48:8–9 and with possible allusion to 58:6.[8] Whether the passage was pre-selected for him or not, there was divine providence "clearly at work in the chosen text."[9]

In summary, the two passages are a clear demonstration of the fact that Jesus had inaugurated the long-awaited kingdom of God and that his disciples and the church in particular had been called to be agents of propagating the message of this kingdom.

Theological Foundation

The kingdom of God must be both theistic and Christological since it is impossible to include God in the debate about His kingdom alongside nontheistic philosophical perspectives. God must be allowed to be who He is—to reign over His creation—or else it would be oxymoronic to talk about the kingdom of God without explicit theistic considerations. The kingdom of God and the gospel it is associated with is about total reconciliation of everything—the cosmos, humans and the entire created order. The concepts of church and the kingdom of God are related, although they tend to be confused, more so when the idea of the "gospel" is included. Indeed, as careful study of the New Testament and church history would show, it is hard to discuss the three concepts separately since they often overlap. Thus, it is common to talk of the *church* as having the responsibility of preaching the *gospel* of the *kingdom of God* and this shows the interrelatedness of the three

6. Arnold, *Bible Backgrounds*, 361.
7. Arnold, *Bible Backgrounds*, 361.
8. Jeffrey, *Luke*, 70.
9. Arnold, *Bible Backgrounds*, 362.

concepts and how their usage is taken for granted within ecclesial circles. But what do these concepts actually mean?

According to John Driver, church is a community of humanity that experiences and communicates God's saving intentions.[10] But what is church and what is its mission? What is the relationship between the church and the kingdom of God? Millard J. Erickson laments that the little debate there is on the subject of church tends to largely revolve around praxis not theologically definitive issues.[11] Answering the question, "what or who is the church?" ought to come first before dealing with the functions the church plays in society and its relationship to the kingdom of God. Instead of giving a clear definition of the church, the Bible rather identifies various "complementary images of the people of God"[12] which helps us to understand what church is before delving into what function this institution plays or is supposed to play in society. Driver ties those biblical images of the church to its mission, and then concludes his book by reminding readers that the church has one mandate: to be an agent of bringing change through, and as a community of transformation.[13]

Cheryl M. Peterson argues that church is not a human creation but rather originates from God who then uses human beings to create it and serve God's mission or *mission dei*.[14] A number of mid-twentieth theologians have advanced a traditional reformation paradigm or the "classic protestant model" of what the church is, notable among which are works of Avery Dulles called *Models of the Church*.[15] Accordingly, this "classic protestant model" holds that the two key ingredients of what constitutes Church are proclamation of the gospel and administration of sacraments. Cheryl M. Peterson's personification of church in the title of her book, "Who is the Church?" confronts the reader with the reality that the Church is a living being with certain functions, a view that aligns with the New Testament image of the Church as a living body—the body of Christ (Romans 12:3–5; 1 Corinthians 12:12–26; Ephesians 1:18–23; Ephesians 5:25–32; Colossians 1:17–20).

From a historical, biblical and theological perspective, the concept of church was not initially a Christian word as such. Within the Greek context, the word simply denoted "a public assembly summoned by a herald," while

10. Driver, *Images of the Church in Mission*, 12.

11. Erickson, *Christian Theology*, 1037.

12. Driver, *Images of the Church in Mission*, 16.

13. Driver, *Images of the Church in Mission*, 16.

14. Peterson, *Who Is the Church?*, 37.

15. Peterson, *Who Is the Church?*, 37.

in the Hebrew usage it brought the idea of a congregation or a gathering of people of Israel.[16] With time, however, the term came to imply that *body politic* associated with followers of Jesus Christ, especially as used in Pauline epistles and in later reference to the growing body of Christian believers. In addition, the church has historically and theologically been defined through creeds as one with four distinct characteristics namely unity, sanctity and holiness, catholicity, and apostolicity.[17] Those characteristics expressly emanate from the Nicene Creed, forming the historic marks of the Church that now serve as key ecclesial pillars of identifying this body of believers.[18]

One reason why the concept of church and its mission is not well understood is because of a lack of a clear distinction between the Church and kingdom of God, especially due to the Roman Catholic Church's traditional view of the two as being synonymous.[19] D. Martyn Lloyd-Jones maintains, however, that the Church is an *expression* of the kingdom since the kingdom is much broader than church.[20] Daniel J. Harrington, on his part, notes that "[W]hile the Church does not replace the kingdom of God, its origin and mission are intimately tied with the kingdom of God" and that "without the kingdom of God as proclaimed by Jesus, the Church has no identity or reason for existence."[21]

Similarly, Jürgen Moltmann's perspective is that, in the longer-range, church is "a way and a transition to the Kingdom of God," thus providing an experiential and a practical life in "eschatological anticipation of the kingdom."[22] Thus, the mission of the church is derived from the mission of God. Although the fall of humanity severed the cordial relationship between humanity and the creator, God instituted a mechanism for restoring that relationship, beginning with Israel, with the intent of forming a special people so as to bring total reconciliation of humans to Himself, to one another and to the rest of creation. This ongoing reconciliation will be fully realized in the future when "God's people will be comforted and reconciled to their creator" culminating with God's salvation reaching even the ends of the earth.[23] Meanwhile, as the church promotes the kingdom of God, individual believers are also continually transformed into effective agents

16. Bromiley, *International Standard Bible Encyclopedia*, 693.
17. Bromiley, *International Standard Bible Encyclopedia*, 694.
18. Kärkkäinen, *Introduction to Ecclesiology.*
19. Lloyd-Jones, *Church and the Last Things*, 3.
20. Lloyd-Jones, *Church and the Last Things*, 4.
21. Harrington, *Church According to the New Testament*, 35.
22. Moltmann, *Church in the Power of the Spirit*, 35.
23. Roberts, "Martin Luther King."

and faithful citizens of that kingdom. That is why Christopher D. Marshall extrapolates this idea by referring to the whole humankind as "God's royal vice-regent in the world."[24]

An appreciation of the kingdom of God must begin with an understanding of who God is, what His mission is and what the mission of His people is. Therefore, when we talk about the kingdom of God, it is about humans allowing God to reign, meaning that people have a great role to play in bringing to bear the kingdom of God. Indeed, the kingdom of God is about God's shalom and his salvation proclaimed through the agency of the church.

Historical Foundation

The church has historically been actively involved in bringing to bear the kingdom of God by presenting the gospel holistically by integrating social and spiritual aspects. At the international level, two prominent personalities are well known in that regard—Dr. David Livingstone (1813—1873) and William Carey (1761–1834). As a medical missionary and explorer to Africa, David Livingstone's contribution to humanity was immense. He contributed to knowledge through geographical discoveries; inspired slave trade abolitionists; helped open up Central Africa for trade, missions, education and healthcare; and facilitated warm relations between local leaders and the British.[25] William Carey, an English Baptist missionary is credited for initiating many successful and life transforming programs in India, prominent among which were Bible translation and production, evangelism, church planting; education, medical relief, social reform, and linguistic and agricultural research.[26]

Here in the United States, one church leader that has greatly shaped the social justice landscape among African-Americans is Reverday C. Ransom (1861–1959), a prominent African-American leader of African Methodist Episcopal Church (A.M.E) who promoted the cause of justice among Americans of color. Ransom is specifically ranked among prominent Black church advocates for social gospel, a movement whose premise was that "Christianity has a social mission to transform the social structures of society in the direction of equality, freedom and community."[27] It has been rightly remarked that Ransom's pioneering work with the social gospel has

24. Marshall, *Crowned with Glory and Honor*, 58.

25. Blaikie, *Personal Life of David Livingstone.*

26. Bebbington, "William Carey," 572.

27. Dorrien, *Social Ethics in the Making*, 60.

enabled Black churches to find "a map for making inroads in the modern scope of human need and potential."[28]

The church has realized the need to ensure that the gospel is relevant and that it addresses challenges of life that believers face in their everyday life. In that regard, discussion on the kingdom of God can sometimes fail to capture the essence of the need to have the experiential part in the here and now without necessarily focusing on the future. This explains why H. Richard Niebuhr is at pains to explain that Jesus' most radical statements in scripture were not closely connected with expectancy of the coming kingdom as such but rather on the realization of "the present rule of God in the course of daily and natural events."[29] So, unless the kingdom of God is seen to have an application and relevance to everyday life and struggles that God's people go through in this life, then the gospel is no good news if all it can promise is a good life in the yonder. Christians of all shades need to have one fundamental conviction: about the nearness of the kingdom of God rather than to its relative ineffectiveness in power and its remoteness in time or space.[30] This is what gives the gospel of the kingdom of God an enduring timeless freshness and relevance to every generation.

Contemporary Foundation

Since the church is the salt of the earth and the light of the world (Mt. 5:13–16) and therefore the agent of the kingdom of God, Christian believers have the mandate to point society to what is right. A lot has been done to inculcate values of the kingdom into the society as part of "gospelling," and that is why J. Jireh Ministries Church is chosen in this project to showcase how church in general ought to be an agent of the kingdom of God. Another example is the Christian Community Development Association (CCDA), an organization that is deeply committed to promotion of social justice among poor people. CCDA inspires, trains, and connects Christians to bear witness to the kingdom of God by reclaiming and restoring under-resourced communities so as to have holistically restored communities, with Christians fully engaged in the process of transformation.[31] Eight principles espoused by CCDA have historically propelled this organization in the quest for social justice. These are (1) *Relocation* (change agents investing in the community by living among the people they are serving. This is incarnation,

28. Pinn, *Making the Gospel Plain*, 5.
29. Niebuhr, *Christ and Culture*, 22.
30. Niebuhr, *Christ and Culture*, 65.
31. "CCD Philosophy." https://ccda.org/about/philosophy/.

taking the example of Jesus who not only "became flesh and blood" but also relocated "into the neighborhood" of humanity (John 1:14—The Message); (2) *Reconciliation* (of people to God and people to people); (3) *Redistribution* of resources as part of justice; (4) *Leadership development* (promotion of local leadership as a long-term investment for sustainable development; (5) *Listening to the community* (by taking into account the thoughts, hopes, dreams, ideas, and aspirations of the community for purposes of finding solutions to their problems and not imposing solutions on them; (6) *Church-based* (the community of God's people is better placed to promote human dignity); (7) *Holistic approach* (going beyond evangelism and discipleship to address the complex needs that define a whole person—social, economic, political, emotional, physical, judicial, educational and familial needs); and (8) *Empowerment* of people (to meet their needs—passing the baton by not doing for people what they can do themselves, thereby becoming proud of what they are doing).

A candid discussion of the kingdom of God and the church has to include the idea of reconciliation. This is because the church is God's agency for reconciling all creation to God. The church therefore, ought to be preoccupied with doing holistic ministry to minister to the entire creation and to reconcile it with the creator. Obviously, this task may not, and will not, achieve the fullness of the expectation of what the ideal kingdom of God would look like, hence the discussion about the kingdom now and the not-yet kingdom.[32]

Improvement of standards of living of a community requires joint collaboration of various stakeholders, including public-private partnerships, nonprofit organizations, and civil society and community groups. Such inclusiveness in doing community work is very crucial because no single individual or organization can improve society single-handedly. In fact, Christian workers must be humble enough to recognize efforts of other entities, most of who may not be Christians and yet are doing the same work of the kingdom.[33] There is therefore need to do genuine partnerships devoid of arrogance on the assumption that Christians are the only ones involved in shaping communities. In that regard, this project will also seek to find out how JJMC's collaboration with other organizations has influenced the local community positively. In particular, it would be good to take note of partnership with government entities on policies relating to social justice since, in Nicholas Wolterstorff's view, governments or state organs have a God-assigned task of exercising governance over the public to curb injustice and encourage justice.[34]

32. Wright, *Surprised by Scripture*, 106.

33. Marsh, *Welcoming Justice*, 100–102.

34. Wolterstorff, *Journey toward Justice*, 199.

God has a stake in justice and therefore definitions of justice must necessarily examine God's view of justice, especially as revealed in Scripture. For example, Hebrew Scriptures depict justice as being about judgment and righteousness, meaning that justice is about "God's *personal passion* for those who lack the basic resources and dignity of life."[35] Just like the example of JJMC, God expects His people to be involved in His mission, and this in turn will enable the church to reflect the image of God or "*Imago Dei.*" But the kingdom of God is not brought about through human effort but rather God's intervention so that the best we can do as a church is to cooperate with God and be in partnership with Him. Indeed, it is God's work accomplished in God's own good time.[36] Thus, human beings are not left out to be "mere spectators on God's work in the world" but rather, their "deeds of justice will act as concrete demonstrations of what God is going to do, and in fact is already doing now, partly through these deeds themselves."[37] This energizes the church to do kingdom work and this is exactly what JJMC is doing in Columbus, OH.

CONTEXT

JJMC is located in a poor neighborhood of Columbus OH where local residents grapple with myriads of social, economic, political and economic challenges. JJMC's call is to minister its congregants while at the same time ministering to the social needs of the local community. The challenge facing JJMC is how to balance between ministering to the hearts of the local community while meeting their physical needs. Two very important questions arise from this challenge: Firstly, how can JJMC go beyond mere provision of handouts to facilitating local residents to acquire life skills that would lead to self-sufficiency and independence? Secondly, how can JJMC link physical/material needs with spiritual connectedness and thereby adopt a holistic approach to ministry? It is possible for JJMC's social programs to become a shining example of how intentional and incarnational ministries in poor urban neighborhoods ought to be run.

The promotion of the gospel of liberation in Latin America by local people is a lesson on how to involve local congregants of JJMC in shaping their community and in dealing with their own social justice issues.[38] Any success in addressing social justice needs can only be measured against the extent to

35. Bruckner, "Justice in Scripture," 4.
36. Marshall, *Crowned with Glory and Honor*, 115.
37. Marshall, *Crowned with Glory and Honor*, 115.
38. Gutiérrez, *We Drink from Our Own Wells.*

which local people are involved so that the results can be both sustainable and be truly "owned" by the people themselves. Marcia A. Owen's case of broad inclusiveness in forums like vigils for victims of violent crimes in Durham (NC) is a good example of stakeholder participation in social justice.[39]

Engagement in strategies for addressing social justice issues for purposes of community building begins with the recognition that something is wrong—that people are suffering and therefore something needs to be done about their situation. However, easy as that might sound, the sheer magnitude of the issue can easily lead to paralysis, despair and cynicism. This can often become a disincentive for not doing anything, especially when one is too careful not to "do the wrong thing in the wrong place at the wrong time in the wrong way for the wrong reasons."[40]

The community where focus of this research project will be is one with myriads issues that require urgent attention. These predominantly AfricanAmericans have historically experienced social and economic injustices due to utilitarian-driven policy decisions that have had adverse implications on the local community. JJMC therefore works hand in hand with other partners to address local injustices with a view to working on solutions that can turn around the fortunes of the residents of this area. This research project will therefore discover what projects JJMC is involved in to help bring God's holistic shalom into this neighborhood and the extent to which JJMC is able to practice the ministry of presence to offer a prophetic voice of hope in a hopeless situation. The aim is to have a restoration of justice, righteousness and total reconciliation—horizontal connectivity (physical poverty included) and vertical connectivity (spiritual poverty).[41]

In addition, this planned project will focus on harmonization of systems and structures of governance, an idea that ties well with what Dorothy C. Bass discusses as the important role played by leadership and governance in terms of ordering, caring for and leading communities.[42] Moreover, as this author adds, "[c]oordinating a community's practices through good governance helps to make its way of life clear, visible, and viable," and this is a good reason why shaping this community of South of Main Street is of utmost importance for the promotion of social justice.[43] Since there are Christians living in this neighborhood, there is need to deal with the perception that Christianity is a mere self-indulgent pietism that lacks

39. Wells and Owen, *Living without Enemies*, 59.

40. Wells and Owen, *Living without Enemies*, 22.

41. Gutiérrez, *We Drink from Our Own Wells*.

42. Bass, *Practicing Our Faith*, 120.

43. Bass, *Practicing Our Faith*, 121.

essential community-building tenets. Thus, Christianity, or Christendom as Charles Marsh would prefer to call it, requires a radical re-evaluation of "personal desires, prejudices, opinions and economic policies in the light of God's moral demands" so that there can be a demonstration of a clear and unwavering concern for the poor, the oppressed, the weak and the helpless in society.[44] This would also include an intentional "public advocacy for economic policies preferential to the poor and oppressed," something that Christians should actually practice over and above verbal proclamation of the kingdom ethos.[45]

It is hoped that this project will discover what answers JJMC provides regarding the plight of the local community and hopefully that will be a lesson on how Christians ought to respond to situations of injustice in society. Through this project, Christians will be empowered and encouraged to play their prophetic role of addressing social injustices, thereby providing valuable lessons on how disciples of Jesus can advocate for social change and restoration of human dignity.[46] Additionally, this project will not only encourage local residents to remain here but that it will also inspire other people to come and be part of the community-building effort like it happened in similar neighborhoods in the American South. In the past, poverty had caused so much flight of young people from poor neighborhoods in the American South to the extent that even after getting good education, none of them wanted to return to their community. However, efforts to woo such people to return and help their community have been one of the clarion calls of John Perkins and his Christian Community Development Association (CCDA) movement, a strategy that is bearing fruit.[47]

Christians are called to address the deep seated spiritual needs that cannot be addressed through other nontheistic social justice programs. Indeed, we are called to build an alternative community.[48] As the salt of the earth and the light of the world (Mt. 5:13–16), the church is called to bring about transformational change in societies by undertaking deliberate and intentional interventions aimed at bringing about positive improvement of communities. This project will find out if this is what JJMC is doing in this needy neighborhood.

44. Marsh, *Welcoming Justice*, 106.

45. Marsh, *Welcoming Justice*, 106.

46. Wolterstorff, *Journey toward Justice*.

47. Perkins, "Cultural Captivity of the Church," 36.

48. Bass, *Practicing Our Faith*, 127.

DEFINITION OF TERMS

Kingdom of God: "the reign of God in human hearts wherever obedience to God is found" and which Christians are expected to spread."[49] *Church*: a Spirit-breathed people who embody forgiveness of sins, formed by the word and sacrament around which they gather to become a *koinonia* of sharing and healing and who are sent into the world to share God's forgiveness and *koinonia* with a hurting and broken world.[50] It is also "a community of humanity that experiences and communicates God's saving intentions."[51]

Mission dei; Latin for mission of God

Imago dei: Latin for Image of God—humans as God's image bearers

PROJECT GOALS

1. To discover participants' understanding of the ministries of J. Jireh Church in their community.
2. To discover the motivations of participants' involvement in J. Jireh Ministries Church.
3. To discover how participants have been personally impacted by J. Jireh
4. Ministries Church.
5. To discover how J. Jireh Ministries Church has impacted the local community
6. To discover how participants experience the presence of God through the presence/ministry of J. Jireh Church.
7. To discover participants' insights on important social issues in this community which need to be addressed.

DESIGN, PROCEDURE, AND ASSESSMENT

It is the purpose of this project to discover how J. Jireh Ministries Church of Columbus, Ohio influences the local community for the kingdom of God. The research question is: How has J. Jireh Ministries Church of Columbus, Ohio influenced the local community for the kingdom of God? The research

49. Erickson, *Christian Theology*, 1163.
50. Adapted from Peterson, *Who Is the Church?*, 147.
51. Driver, *Images of the Church in Mission*, 12.

design of this project is both a quantitative and qualitative study aimed at soliciting answers to close-ended and open-ended questions respectively. Questions will be directed to members of the local community comprising members as well as nonmembers of the congregation of JJMC. Interview schedules will be prepared and subsequently administered personally by the researcher with possible assistance of a research assistant. The target is to gather survey data from a minimum of 20 respondents who will help tell the story of the extent to which JJMC has impacted the lives of the local community directly and indirectly. Individual and group narratives will contribute towards the larger narrative that will help tell the story of the extent to which the local community has been influenced positively by JJMC i in ushering in the kingdom of God and its ethos.

This research project will have close interaction with the leadership of JJMC who will provide a detailed narrative of the background of the church's presence in this community and the subsequent collaborative initiatives that have been forged to address social and economic justice issues in this neighborhood.

Drawing participants from within and outside the membership of JJMC will help provide diversity and inclusiveness that will be necessary to discover actual impact of the church in the community where its physical presence is felt. The survey instrument will cover a number of issues including demographics, length of residence in the neighborhood and church-initiated activities and practices in the neighborhood. This study is not intended to subject information collected to statistical analysis, and that means that no correlations and comparisons will be drawn from the data collected. The survey will end with a "thank you" section to show gratitude to participants for consenting to answer questions in the survey.

PERSONAL GOALS

On the whole, my choice of a project on social justice is propelled by what I consider to be my calling. Frederick Buechner's words are particularly appropriate in this regard: "The place God calls you to is the Place where your deep gladness and the world's deep hunger meet."[52] Specifically, there are four personal goals that I hope to accomplish during this study:

1. I would like to be able to be educated on what my role is in the Church as far as kingdom of God is concerned;

52. Buechner, *Wishful Thinking*, 119.

2. I would like to learn from others how to be effective in the kingdomoriented ministry of reconciliation;
3. I would like to be equipped to train others to be kingdom-oriented in the ministry of reconciliation; and
4. At the end of the study I would like to launch a full-fledged kingdomoriented ministry of reconciliation that promotes issues covered in this project.

CALENDAR

YEAR	DATE/MONTH	ACTIVITY
2015	July 3	Project proposal completed and submitted.
2015	July 3—October 31	Project Approval process
2015	August—September	Reading and collecting library information
2015	October	Attend writing seminar and develop/polish draft research instruments
2015	November	Preparation of Research instruments
2015	December	Fine-tune the research instruments
2016	January	Administration of Research instruments
2016	February	Evaluate and analyze results of the data
2016	March	Write Chapter 2 and submit to advisor
2016	April	Write Chapter 3 and submit to advisor
2016	May	Write Chapter 4 and submit to advisor
2016	June	Write chapter 5 and submit to advisor
2016	July	Write Chapter 6 and submit to advisor
2016	August 15	Write Chapter 1 and submit to advisor
2016	August 30	Write Preliminaries & Reference List and submit to advisor
2016	September	Submit Final dissertation
2016	October	Defense
2016	December	Graduation

CORE TEAM

Advisor: Dr. Wyndy Corbin Reuschling

Professor of Ethics and Theology, Ashland Theological Seminary, Ashland, Ohio

Field consultant/Advisor: Rev. Norman Brown, Executive Director J. Jireh

Ministries Church, Columbus Ohio

RESOURCE PERSONS:

Rev. Vivian Brown, Pastor of J. Jireh Ministries Church, Columbus OH

Rev. Dan Franz, Urban Ministry, Vineyard Church, Columbus OH

Chris Jones, Church and Social Justice Consultant, Irwin, OH

Robert Caldwell Jr., Executive Director, Poverty Matters, Columbus OH

SUPPORT TEAM

Rob Swartz, Pastor of London Christian Fellowship, London Ohio

Reuben Sairs, Librarian, Rosedale Bible College, Irwin, OH

Naomy Ndungu, my wife—Irwin, OH

LIFE MANAGEMENT PLAN

Management of finances is a major factor of consideration in my seminary journey, especially considering that a large part of my studies has been funded with loans which are soon becoming due. I have therefore to decide how I am going to juggle between completing my studies and repaying those loans. This will call for a change in my lifestyle. Towards this end, I intend to look for a job or jobs that will pay well and which will also allow me to devote time for doing research and writing my dissertation. If the worse comes to the worst, I may have to at the least begin making payments on interests for those loans so that I do not default on both the principal and the interest amounts.

One of my strengths in time management is that I wake up early and also tend to concentrate on what I am doing for a considerable length of time. I plan to use this strength to work for my good so that on the days I will not be going for work, I intend to begin carrying out dissertation-related activities early. A clear week-by-week time table will greatly help in this regard. One of my weaknesses, however, is that once I get it is hard I must take a break. May be this is not a weakness as such since a break is as good as a rest, so the saying goes. But once I take a break I am able to concentrate again for a considerable period of time. Personally, there is a lot of demand on my time between the family (nuclear and extended), work and now studies. Although balancing all these demands is not easy, I plan on ensuring neither of these demands is ignored. One way might be revising my financial commitments so that I do not have to work for long hours in order to have time for studies and family, both of which are important.

Besides time management, I plan to revamp my organizational skills by putting on the door of our kitchen refrigerator a timetable for seminary-related work as well as family, work and personal matters. I may have to create a folder in my computer that will contain summaries of assignments and their due dates so that I can always peep and see what activity should be carried out when. This organization will certainly help me to not get late in turning in dissertation work to my advisor or to fail to honor important research-related appointments. I will also have a schedule for other commitments outside seminary, including family, church, work and other engagements that will require my attention. That way, I will be able to complete my research work and write the dissertation smoothly.

An area that will require my attention is getting time for recreation, rest and leisure. I realize that one's health can be greatly affected by lifestyles that do not give the body and the mind time to relax. I will have to work on this, including allocating time to prayer, meditation and studying the word of God for personal growth. It is through such moments of spiritual retreats that God can speak to me and help me to not only do my studies but also be spiritually alert to whatever He would like to do with and in my life.

Appendix 2

Questionnaire

COVER LETTER

My name is Abraham Ndungu, a doctoral candidate at Ashland Theological Seminary in Ashland, OH. Thank you for agreeing to participate in this project survey which seeks your opinions regarding how J. Jireh Ministries' presence has influenced this community and how its ministry can be improved. Your participation in this survey is purely voluntary and the information you provide will be treated with confidence. Results of the study will be given to you, if you request.

Again, thank you for participating in this study.
ABRAHAM NDUNGU

Present age (*circle one*):

18–25
26–30
31–35
36–40
41–45
46–50
51–55
56–60
61–65
66–70
71–75
More than 75

Gender:

Male
Female

Number of years you have lived in or associated with this South of Main Street neighborhood? *(circle one):*

Less than a year 1–2 3–4 5–6 7–8 9–10 Over 10

Number of years you have associated with J. Jireh Ministries? (*circle one*).

Less than a year 1–2 3–4 5–6 7–8 9–10 Over 10

Please read each statement below and circle the response that best describes your opinion.

- Strongly Disagree
- Somewhat Disagree
- Neutral
- Somewhat Agree
- Strongly Agree

I know what J. Jireh Ministries does in this neighborhood.

1 2 3 4 5

I am involved in J. Jireh Ministries because I saw the good work they do.

1 2 3 4 5

I am involved in J. Jireh Ministries because I was invited into participation.

1 2 3 4 5

J. Jireh Ministries has helped me personally.

1 2 3 4 5

J. Jireh Ministries does community work in South of Main Street neighborhood.

1 2 3 4 5

Please read each statement below and circle the response that best describes your opinion.

Strongly Disagree
Somewhat Disagree
Neutral
Somewhat Agree
Strongly Agree

I have witnessed the way J. Jireh Ministries has helped the community Of South of Main.

1 2 3 4 5

I have learned from other people how J. Jireh Ministries has helped the community of South of Main.

1 2 3 4 5

I am satisfied with the current community/social programs run by J. Jireh Ministries.

1 2 3 4 5

J. Jireh Ministries would do better by introducing other social programs in which it is was not currently involved.

1 2 3 4 5

J. Jireh Ministries has helped members of my family.

1 2 3 4 5

J. Jireh Ministries has helped me to continue to deepen my spirituality.

1 2 3 4 5

I have experienced the presence of God during my participation in J. Jireh Ministry program of activities.

1 2 3 4 5

Instructions: in the following questions, please give a brief response. If you need more space, please add a page.
List two (2) ministry programs run by J. Jireh Ministries in the community of South of Main Street that you are familiar with.

Explain what attracted you to J. Jireh Ministries.

If J. Jireh Ministries has been of help to the local community of South of Main, describe two (2) ways in which this has happened.

List other two (2) ways in which J. Jireh Ministries can improve its current ministry in the community of South of Main.

Please discuss how J. Jireh Ministries has helped you and/or your family.

Explain ways in which you experience the presence of God in J. Jireh Ministries Church.

Suggest two (2) programs J. Jireh Ministries Church is not currently undertaking in South of Main neighborhood that could benefit the community.

Thank you for your participation.

Appendix 3

Background and Ministries of J. Jireh Ministries Church

BACKGROUND OF J. JIREH MINISTRIES

In 2000, Rev. Norman J. Brown already had an architectural design firm, but included a construction management and construction services to his company. At the time, 50 percent of his construction crew was comprised of "restored citizens." One of his employees was living in a half-way house and he informed Rev. Brown that he wanted to give his life back to the Lord and get baptized. Rev. Brown asked if he could do a Bible study with him. He wanted to make sure the employee understood the meaning of water baptism. The employee got permission from the staff of the half-way house to study the Bible with Rev. Brown. When Rev. Brown arrived at the half-way house, the employee had invited four other residents to sit in on the Bible study. When the Bible study started, Rev. Brown asked all of the men to read some of the Scriptures and began to realize that a few of the men could not read. Therefore, Rev. Brown established a literacy program in the half-way house and also brought video tapes to watch other ministers preach at men's gatherings.

This is where Rev. Brown started J. Jireh Ministries Church, in a half-way house for men. In 2003, when these men left the half-way house, they and others would gather in the living room of the home of Norman and Vivian Brown for worship services. In the beginning, J. Jireh Ministries Church had two locations: at the home of Norman and Vivian Brown and at the halfway house for the restored citizens. Rev. Brown used his construction company as a way to provide employment opportunities and minister to the men on the construction site. Rev. Brown would invest in his employees by purchasing books for them to read for spiritual and personal growth.

J. JIREH MINISTRIES PROGRAM OF ACTIVITIES

An Overview

JJMC does not have a "pre-packaged" set of ministries which are waiting for people to join. Rather, JJMC disciples and encourages people to "walk" in their grace. Its activities include the following: church (mainly weekly services and Bible studies; benevolence, visitations, prayers and related pastoral concerns; a program called "Kingdom Institute"); a Youth Summer Enrichment Program; a Video Game Night; the Kimball Farms Community Garden; community love feasts (or block parties); community cleanups; National Night Out; convening and hosting monthly civic association meetings; community food pantry and distribution; community health fairs; addressing drug/alcohol issues; addressing community crime/violence issues by holding peace liaison meetings; addressing community unemployment through job fairs; promoting blood donation to the American Red Cross; addressing poor educational systems at two neighborhood schools (one elementary and one middle school); renovation of existing neighborhood houses for ex-offenders and veterans; ministering to three needy groups of ex-offenders or "restored citizens," veterans, and "at-risk" youth; and working with suburban and urban local churches to bring the kingdom of God to the community.

DETAILED MINISTRIES

1. Church

    - Mainly weekly (Saturday night) church services and Tuesday night Bible studies
    - *Everyone* in JJMC is strongly encouraged to use their spiritual gifts as a ministry within the structure of JJMC. Whoever has a spiritual gift, that person is discipled to use their spiritual gifts as a ministry of JJMC.
    - Benevolence, visitations, prayers, and related pastoral concerns.

- A program called "J. Jireh Ministry Kingdom Institute."

2. Youth Summer Enrichment Program—for the children living in the Community of Kimball Farms and Franklin County Children Services.
3. Establishment of Kimball Farms Community Garden, East Main Street: to teach the children about health/wellness. They will eat and sell what they are growing. A volunteer from Westerville and The Ohio State University Extension has been working with our children in developing the garden. Our plan is to transfer the gardening experience into math, science, reading, health, and business development.
4. Commissioned two studies by The Ohio State University.

    - A revitalization Plan—The Future of JJMC in Revitalization of the Local Neighborhood: Options available: Collaboration with local authorities and Identification of resources
    - A Comprehensive Development Plan on future of The Community of Kimball Farms.

5. Community Love Feasts or Block Parties—besides providing food, fun, movies, and video games, this event addresses neighborhood pride, health/wellness, crime, and diet/nutrition.
6. Community Cleanups.
7. National Night Outs.
8. South of Main Civic Association (SOMCA) meetings; now called Kimball Farms Civic Association—convening and hosting monthly civic association meetings.
9. Mid-Ohio Food Bank to provide fresh produce to The Community of Kimball Farms.
10. Community Health Fairs.
11. Partnering with Mt Carmel Hospital and the Columbus Health Department to bring their resources to the community to address health and wellness issues.
12. ADAMH Board to address drug/alcohol issues.
13. The Columbus Police Department and the Columbus Fire Department to address community crime/violence Issues.
14. COWIC and Henkels & McCoy Training Center to address high community unemployment.

15. American Red Cross for the need of new blood.
16. Two neighborhood schools (one elementary and one middle school) to address the poor educational systems.
17. Working with suburban and urban local churches to bring the kingdom of God to the community.
18. Health and Wellness programs.
19. Food and Clothing Pantry.
20. Renovation of existing houses for "restored citizens" and veterans.
21. Holding Peace Liaison meetings.
22. Addressing unemployment issues though job fairs.
23. Ministering to three needy groups: ex-offenders or restored citizens, veterans, and "at-risk" youth.
24. Partnering with the Columbus Health Department to provide a "Community Connector" to address the high rate of infant mortality within the community.
25. Urban Farming: In the late 1800's, this neighborhood was known as Kimball Farms. The Kimball Farms Community Garden, East Main Street has been developed to become the first of many other community gardens and/or "urban" farms in our neighborhood. Our goal is to establish a community garden or an "urban" farm on every street in this neighborhood. These garden projects address the six chronic issues within this community: poor education, poor housing, poor health/wellness, poor public safety, poor employment, and poor economy. J. Jireh Development Corp. (JJDC), one of the ministries of JJMC, has renovated four houses within the neighborhood and each house has a community garden. Both, JJMC and JJDC have qualified to obtain a greenhouse from the US Department of Agriculture. The new greenhouses will be located at 1676 East Main Street and 607 Kelton Avenue. To be constructed by October 2016, these new greenhouses will provide the opportunity to grow produce 12 months of the year; these sites are called "urban" farms due the job creation ventures. These garden projects are addressing nutrition/wellness, food production, children's education, and job training by changing a culture and a paradigm within this neighborhood.

Bibliography

"About the Action Institute: Our Mission & Core Principles." *Acton Institute*. Accessed April 2, 2017. https://www.acton.org/about/mission.

"About the Action Institute: History of the Acton Institute." *Acton Institute*. Accessed October 15, 2016. http://www.acton.org/about/history-acton-institute.

Adeney-Riskotta, Bernard T. *Strange Virtues: Ethics in a Multicultural World*. Downers Grove, IL: InterVarsity Press, 1995.

Arnold, Clinton E., ed. *Zondervan Illustrated Bible Backgrounds Commentary*. Grand Rapids: Zondervan, 2002.

Augustine. *The Confessions of St. Augustine, Bishop of Hippo*. Translated by Edward B. Pusey. New York: P.F. Collier & Son, 1909.

Bacote, Vincent. "Social Justice and Christian Obedience: Present and Future Challenges." In *The Church's Social Responsibility: Reflections on Evangelicalism and Social Justice*, edited by Jordan J. Ballor et al., 1469–1568. Grand Rapids: Christian's Library, 2016. Kindle.

Bailey, Kenneth E. *Jesus through Middle Eastern Eyes: Cultural Studies in the Gospels*. Downers Grove, IL: InterVarsity, 2008.

Balentine, Samuel E. "He Unrolled the Scroll . . . and He Rolled Up the Scroll and Gave It Back." *Cross Currents* 59, no. 2 (June 2009) 154–175.

Ballor, Jordan J., and Robert Joustra. "Introduction: The Evangelical Church's Social Responsibility." In *The Church's Social Responsibility: Reflections on Evangelicalism and Social Justice*, edited by Jordan J. Ballor et al., 51–201. Grand Rapids: Christian's Library, 2016. Kindle.

Bass, Diana Butler. *A People's History of Christianity: The Other Side of the Story*. New York: HarperOne, 2009. Kindle.

Bass, Dorothy C., ed. *Practicing Our Faith: A Way of Life for a Searching People*. San Francisco: Jossey-Bass, 1997.

Bass, D., and C. Dykstra. "A Theological Understanding of Christian Practices." In *Practicing Theology: Beliefs and Practices in Christian Life*, edited by Miroslav Volf et al., 13–31. Grand Rapids: Eerdmans, 2002.

Bebbington, D.W. "William Carey." In *Introduction to the History of Christianity*, rev. ed., edited by Tim Dowley, 572. Minneapolis: Fortress, 2002.

Bediako, Kwame. *Jesus and the Gospel in Africa: History and Experience*. Maryknoll, NY: Orbis, 2004.

Blackaby, Henry T., and Claude V. King. *Experiencing God: How to Live the Full Adventure of Knowing and Doing the Will of God*. Nashville: B&H, 1998.

Blaikie, William Garden. *The Personal Life of David Livingstone*. NY: Dossier, 2004.

Block, Peter, et al. *An Other Kingdom: Departing the Consumer Culture*. Hoboken, NJ: Wiley, 2016.

Bohi, Janette. "A Lentz." In *Introduction to the History of Christianity*, rev. ed., edited by Tim Dowley, 544–547. Minneapolis: Fortress, 2002.

Bosnich, David A. "The Principle of Subsidiarity." *Acton Institute Religion and Liberty Journal* 6, no. 4 (August 1996) 9–10.

Boyd, Gregory A. *The Myth of a Christian Religion: Losing Your Religion for the Beauty of a Revolution*. Grand Rapids: Zondervan, 2009.

Brock, Peter, and Nigel Young. *Pacifism in the Twentieth Century*. Syracuse, NY: Syracuse University Press, 1999.

Bromiley, Geoffrey W. *International Standard Bible Encyclopedia: A–D*, rev. ed. Grand Rapids: Eerdmans, 1979.

Brown, Jeannine K., et al. *Becoming Whole and Holy: An Integrative Conversation about Christian Formation*. Grand Rapids: Baker Academic, 2011.

Bruckner, James. "Justice in Scripture." *Ex Auditu* 22 (2006) 1–9.

Brueggemann, Walter. *The Prophetic Imagination: Preaching an Emancipatory Word*. Minneapolis: Fortress, 2001.

Buechner, Frederick. *Wishful Thinking: A Seeker's ABC*, rev. ed. San Fransisco: HarperOne, 1993.

Cairns, Earle E. *Christianity through the Centuries: A History of the Christian Church*. Grand Rapids: Zondervan, 1981.

Cannon, Mae Elise. *Social Justice Handbook: Small Steps for a Better World*. Downers Grove, IL: InterVarsity, 2009.

Castellanos, Noel. *Where the Cross Meets the Street: What Happens to the Neighborhood When God Is at the Center*. Downers Grove, IL: InterVarsity, 2015. Kindle.

"CCD Philosophy." *Christian Community Development Association*. Accessed September 12, 2016. https://ccda.org/about/philosophy/.

Cho, Eugene. *Overrated: Are We More in Love with the Idea of Changing the World Than Actually Changing the World?* Colorado Springs: David C. Cook, 2014. Kindle.

Claar, Victor V., and Robin Kendrick Klay. *Economics in Christian Perspective: Theory, Policy and Life Choices*. Downers Grove, IL: InterVarsity, 2007.

Cleveland, Christena. *Disunity in Christ: Uncovering the Hidden Forces that Keep Us Apart*. Downers Grove, IL: InterVarsity, 2013.

Dayton, Donald W. *Discovering an Evangelical Heritage*. Reprint. Peabody, MA: Baker Academic, 1988.

De Santis, V.P. "Civil Rights." In Vol. 3, *New Catholic Encyclopedia*. Washington, DC: McGraw-Hill, 1967.

DeYoung, Kevin, and Greg Gilbert. *What Is the Mission of the Church?: Making Sense of Social Justice, Shalom, and the Great Commission*. Wheaton, IL: Crossway, 2011.

Dorrien, Gary. *Social Ethics in the Making: Interpreting an American Tradition*. Malden, MA: Wiley-Blackwell, 2010.

Douglas, J.D. "Ambassador." In *New Bible Dictionary*, 3rd ed., edited by Howard I. Marshall et al. Leicester, England: InterVarsity, 1996.

Driesenga, Jessica. "A Pearl and a Leaven: The Twofold Call of the Gospel." In *The Church's Social Responsibility: Reflections on Evangelicalism and Social Justice*, edited by Jordan J. Ballor et al., 586–687. Grand Rapids: Christian's Library, 2016. Kindle.

Driver, John. *Images of the Church in Mission*. Scottdale, PA: Herald, 1997.

Dulles, Avery. *Models of the Church*. New York: Random, 2002.

Dunn, James. "Pentecostalism and the Charismatic Movement." In *Introduction to the History of Christianity*, rev. ed., edited by Tim Dowley, 646–650. Minneapolis: Fortress, 2002.

Dykstra, Craig, and Dorothy C. Bass. "Times of Yearning, Practices of Faith." In *Practicing Our Faith: A Way of Life for a Searching People*, edited by Dorothy C. Bass, 1–12. San Francisco: Jossey-Bass, 1997.

Erickson, Millard J. *Christian Theology*, 2nd ed. Grand Rapids: Baker Academic, 1998.

Fitch, David E., and Geoff Holsclaw. *Prodigal Christianity: 10 Signposts into the Missional Frontier*. Peabody, MA: Jossey-Bass, 2013. Kindle.

Flatt, Kevin N. "Historical Epilogue: A Cautionary Tale." In *The Church's Social Responsibility: Reflections on Evangelicalism and Social Justice*, edited by Jordan J. Ballor et al., 1592–1690. Grand Rapids: Christian's Library, 2016. Kindle.

Florence, Anna Carter. *Inscribing the Text: Sermons and Prayers of Walter Brueggemann*. Minneapolis: Fortres, 2011.

France, R.T. *Luke*. Teach the Text Commentary Series. Grand Rapids: Baker Academic, 2013.

Gloer, W. Hullit. "Ambassadors of Reconciliation: Paul's Genius in Applying the Gospel in a Multi-Cultural World: 2 Corinthians 5:14–21." *Ambassadors of Reconciliation Review and Expositor* 104 (Summer 2007) 589–601.

Grenz, Stanley J., et al. *Pocket Dictionary of Theological Terms*. Downers Grove, IL: InterVarsity, 1999.

Gula, Richard M. *The Call to Holiness: Embracing a Fully Christian Life*. New York: Paulist, 2003

Gutiérrez, Gustavo. *We Drink from Our Own Wells: The Spiritual Journey of a People*, 20th ed. Maryknoll, NY: Orbis, 2003.

Hardman, Keith J. *Charles Grandison Finney, 1792–1875: Revivalist and Reformer*. Grand Rapids: Baker, 1990.

Harrington, Daniel J. *The Church according to the New Testament: What the Wisdom and Witness of Early Christianity Teach Us Today*. Franklin, WI: Sheed and Ward, 2001.

Harrison, Eugene Myers. *Giants of Missionary Trail*. North Fort Myers, FL: Faithful Life, 2010.

Hays, Richard B. *The Moral Vision of the New Testament: Community, Cross, New Creation: A Contemporary Introduction to New Testament Ethics*. New York: HarperCollins, 1990.

———. "Scripture-Shaped Community: The Problem of Method in New Testament Ethics." *Interpretation* 44, no. 1 (1990) 42–55.

———. "The Word of Reconciliation." *Faith and Leadership* (blog), July 19, 2010. https://faithandleadership.com/word-reconciliation.

Hogeterp, Mike. "Why the Church Must Not Stay Silent: Liturgy and the Legacy of Colonialism." In *The Church's Social Responsibility: Reflections on Evangelicalism and Social Justice*, edited by Jordan J. Ballor et al., 1094–1143. Grand Rapids: Christian's Library, 2016. Kindle.

Horton, James Oliver, and Lois E. Horton. *Slavery and the Making of America*. Oxford: Oxford University Press, 2006.

Horvat, John, II. *Return to Order: From a Frenzied Economy to an Organic Christian Society: Where We've Been, How We Got Here, and Where We Need to Go*. York, PA: York, 2013. Kindle.

Jahn, Gunnar. "Award Ceremony Speech: Presentation Speech by Gunnar Jahn, Chairman of the Nobel Committee on 10 December 1964." *Nobel Media*. October 7, 2020. http://www.nobelprize.org/nobel_prizes/peace/laureates/1964/press.html.

Jeffrey, David Lyle. *Luke: Brazos Theological Commentary on the Bible*. Grand Rapids: Brazos, 2012.

Jensen, Robin. "Baptismal Rights and Architecture." In *Late Ancient Christianity*, edited by Virginia Burrus. Minneapolis: Fortress, 2005.

Johnstone, Patrick. *The Future of the Global Church: History, Trends and Possibilities*. Colorado Springs: Biblica, 2011.

Kärkkäinen, Veli-Matti. *Introduction to Ecclesiology: Ecumenical, Historical and Global Perspectives*. Downers Grove, IL: InterVarsity, 2002.

Keller, Timothy. *The Prodigal God: Recovering the Heart of the Christian Faith*. New York: Penguin, 2008.

King, Martin Luther, Jr. *Strength to Love*. Minneapolis: Fortress, 1981.

Klein, Lisa M. *Be It Remembered: The Story of Trinity Episcopal Church on Capitol Square, Columbus, Ohio*. Wilmington, OH: Orange Frazer, 2003.

Ladd, George Eldon. *The Presence of the Future: The Eschatology of Biblical Realism*, rev. ed. Grand Rapids: Eerdmans, 1996.

Lentz, Ed. *Columbus: The Story of a City*. The Making of America Series. Charleston, SC: Arcadia, 2003.

Levison, J.R. "Creation and New Creation." In *Dictionary of Paul and His Letters*, edited by Gerald F. Hawthorne et al. Downers Grove, IL: InterVarsity, 1993.

Lloyd-Jones, D. Martyn. *The Church and the Last Things*. Wheaton, IL: Crossway, 1998.

Marsh, Charles, and John M. Perkins. *Welcoming Justice: God's Movement toward Beloved Community*. Downers Grove, IL: InterVarsity, 2009.

Marshall, Christopher D. *Crowned with Glory and Honor: Human Rights in the Biblical Tradition*. Auckland, NZ: Herald, 2003.

Mayer, Robert H., ed. *The Civil Rights Act of 1964*. 40 vols. San Diego: Greenhaven, 2004.

McGrath, Alister E. *Christianity's Dangerous Idea: The Protestant Revolution—A History from the Sixteenth Century to the Twenty-First*. New York: HarperCollins, 2007.

McKnight, Scot. *A Community Called Atonement*. Nashville, TN: Abingdon, 2007.

———. *Kingdom Conspiracy: Returning to the Radical Mission of the Local Church*. Grand Rapids: Brazos, 2014.

McQuilkin, Robertson. *An Introduction to Biblical Ethics*, rev. ed. Wheaton, IL: Tyndale, 1995.

Mead, Loren B. *The Once and Future Church: Reinventing the Congregation for a New Mission Frontier*. The Once and Future Church Series. New York: Rowman & Littlefield, 1991.

Moltmann, Jürgen. *The Church in the Power of the Spirit: A Contribution to Messianic Ecclesiology.* 1st ed. Minneapolis: Fortress, 1993.

Mouw, Richard J. "Carl Henry Was Right." In *The Church's Social Responsibility: Reflections on Evangelicalism and Social Justice*, edited by Jordan J. Ballor et al., 453–547. Grand Rapids: Christian's Library, 2016. Kindle.

Murray, Stuart. *The Naked Anabaptist: The Bare Essentials of a Radical Faith.* Scottdale, PA: Herald, 2010.

NC Forward Together Moral Movement Channel. "We Must Raise a Moral Dissent! | William J. Barber, II." YouTube video. August 20, 2013. https://www.youtube.com/watch?v=8VTwgZw_wuM.

Niebuhr, H. Richard. *Christ and Culture.* New York: Harper & Row, 1956.

———. *The Kingdom of God in America.* Middletown, CT: Wesleyan, 1988.

Noll, Mark A. *God and Race in American Politics: A Short History.* Princeton, NJ: Princeton University Press, 2008.

O'Day, Gail R. "Today This Word Is Fulfilled in Your Hearing: A Scriptural Hermeneutic of Biblical Authority." *Word & World* 26, no. 4 (Fall 2006) 357–364.

Palmer, Parker J. *Healing the Heart of Democracy: The Courage to Create a Politics Worthy of the Human Spirit.* San Francisco: Jossey-Bass, 2011.

Paul, John, II. *Centesimus Annus: On the Hundredth Anniversary of Rerum Novarum.* Encyclical Letter. Vatican website. May 1, 1991. http://www.vatican.va/content/john-paul-ii/en/encyclicals/documents/hf_jp-ii_enc_01051991_centesimus-annus.html.

Peterson, Cheryl M. *Who Is the Church?: An Ecclesiology for the Twenty-First Century.* Minneapolis: Fortress, 2013.

Piedra, Alberto M. *Natural Law: The Foundation of an Orderly Economic System.* Lanham, MD: Lexington, 2004.

Rah, Soong-Chan, and Gary VanderPol. *Return to Justice: Six Movements That Reignited Our Contemporary Evangelical Conscience.* Grand Rapids: Brazos, 2016.

Ransom, Reverdy C. *Making the Gospel Plain: The Writings of Bishop Reverdy C. Ransom.* Edited by Anthony B. Pinn. Harrisburg, PA: T&T Clark, 1999.

Rasmussen, Larry. "Shaping Communities." In *Practicing Our Faith: A Way of Life for a Searching People*, edited by Dorothy C. Bass. 119–132. San Francisco: Jossey-Bass, 1997.

Reed, Esther D. *The Ethics of Human Rights: Contested Doctrinal and Moral Issues.* Waco, TX: Baylor University Press, 2007.

Reuschling, Wyndy Corbin. *Desire for God and the Things of God: The Relationships between Christian Spirituality and Morality.* Eugene, OR: Cascade, 2012.

———. "Christian Ethical Commitments in the Kingdom of God." In *Celebrations and Convictions: Honoring the Life and Legacy of Dr. Luke L. Keefer, Jr.*, edited by J. Robert Douglass et al., 213–228. Mechanicsburg, PA: Brethren in Christ Historical Society, 2015.

Richards, Lawrence O. *Zondervan Expository Dictionary of Bible Words.* Grand Rapids: Zondervan, 1991.

Roberts, Mark D. "The Mission of God and the Missional Church." *Mark D. Roberts: Reflections on Christ, Church, & Culture* (blog). January 12, 2009. http://www.patheos.com/blogs/markdroberts/series/the-mission-of-god-and-the-missional-church/.

Roberts, Wesley A. "Martin Luther King." In *Introduction to the History of Christianity*, rev. ed, edited by Tim Dowley, 606. Minneapolis: Fortress, 2002.

Roxburgh, Alan J. *Missional: Joining God in the Neighborhood.* Grand Rapids: Baker, 2011.

Salvatierra, Alexia, and Peter Heltzel. *Faith-Rooted Organizing: Mobilizing the Church in Service to the World.* Downers Grove, IL: InterVarsity, 2014.

Schaeffer, Francis A. *Pollution and the Death of Man: The Creation View of Ecology.* Wheaton, IL: Tyndale, 1970.

Schreiber, Franziska, and Alexander Carius. "The Inclusive City: Urban Planning for Diversity and Social Cohesion." In *Can a City Be Sustainable?*, edited by Gary Gardner et al., 6631–7137. Washington, DC: Island, 2016. Kindle.

Shaw, Mark. *Global Awakening: How 20th-Century Revivals Triggered a Christian Revolution.* Downers Grove, IL: InterVarsity, 2010.

Shelley, Bruce L. *Church History in Plain Language.* Nashville, TN: Thomas Nelson, 2008.

Sherman, Amy L. *Kingdom Calling: Vocational Stewardship for the Common Good.* Downers Grove, IL: InterVarsity, 2011.

Sider, Ronald J., Philip N. Olson, and Heidi Rolland Unruh. *Churches That Make a Difference: Reaching Your Community with Good News and Good Works.* Grand Rapids: Baker, 2002.

Sider, Ronald J. *Good News and Good Works: A Theology for the Whole Gospel.* Grand Rapids: Baker, 1999.

Sirico, Robert. *A Moral Basis for Liberty*, 3rd ed. Grand Rapids: Acton Institute, 2012.

Smith, James K.A. *Who's Afraid of Postmodernism?: Taking Derrida, Lyotard, and Foucault to Church.* The Church and Postmodern Culture. Grand Rapids: Baker Academic, 2006.

Snodgrass, Klyne R. "Reconciliation: God Being God with Special Reference to 2 Cor. 5:11–6:4." *Covenant Quarterly* 60, no. 2 (May 2002) 323.

Snyder, Howard A., and Daniel V. Runyon. *Decoding the Church: Mapping the DNA of Christ's Body.* Grand Rapids: Baker Academic, 2002.

Snyder, Howard A. *Models of the Kingdom.* Nashville, TN: Abingdon, 1991.

Spohn, William. *Go and Do Likewise: Jesus and Ethics.* New York: Bloomsbury Academic, 2000.

Stamm, M.W. "Liturgy and Worship." In *Global Dictionary of Theology: A Resource for the Worldwide Church*, edited by William Dyrness et al., . Downers Grove, IL: InterVarsity, 2008.

Stearns, Richard. *The Hole in Our Gospel: What Does God Expect of Us? The Answer That Changed My Life and Might Just Change the World.* Nashville, TN: Thomas Nelson, 2009.

Stott, John R. *Christian Mission in the Modern World.* Downers Grove, IL: InterVarsity, 1975.

Suderman, Robert J. "Reflections on Anabaptist Ecclesiology." In *Living Christian Life in Today's World: A Conversation Between Mennonite World Conference and the Seventh-day Adventist Church, 2011–2012*, edited by Carol E. Rasmussen, . Silver Spring, MD: General Conference of Seventh-day Adventists, 2014.

Um, Stephen T., and Justin Buzzard. *Why Cities Matter: To God, the Culture, and the Church.* Wheaton, IL: Crossway, 2013.

Wagenman, Michael R. "Abraham Kuyper, the Institutional Church, and Socio-Political Engagement." In *The Church's Social Responsibility: Reflections on Evangelicalism and Social Justice*, edited by Jordan J. Ballor et al., 802–890. Grand Rapids: Christian's Library, 2016. Kindle.

Wagner, C. Peter, et al. *Church Growth: State of the Art*. Wheaton, IL: Tyndale, 1986.

Walton, John H. *The Lost World of Genesis One: Ancient Cosmology and the Origins Debate*. Downers Grove, IL: InterVarsity, 2009.

Washington, James Melvin. *A Testament of Hope: The Essential Writings and Speeches of Martin Luther King Jr.* San Francisco: HarperOne, 1991.

Wells, Samuel, and Marcia A. Owen. *Living without Enemies: Being Present in the Midst of Violence*. Downers Grove, IL: InterVarsity, 2011.

Wills, David. "Reverdy C. Ransom: The Making of an A.M.E. Bishop." In *Black Apostles: Afro-American Clergy Confront the Twentieth Century*, edited by Randall K. Burdett, . Boston: G.K. Hall, 1978.

Wolterstorff, Nicholas P. "The Contours of Justice: An Ancient Call for Shalom." In *God and the Victim: Theological Reflections on Evil, Victimization, Justice, and Forgiveness*, edited by Lisa Barnes Lampman, 107–130. Grand Rapids: Eerdmans, 1999.

———. *Journey toward Justice: Personal Encounters in the Global South*. Grand Rapids: Baker Academic, 2013.

Wright, N.T. *The Case for the Psalms: Why They Are Essential*. New York: HarperOne, 2013. Kindle.

———. *The Day the Revolution Began: Reconsidering the Meaning of Jesus's Crucifixion*. New York: HarperCollins, 2016.

———. *How God Became King: The Forgotten Story of the Gospels*. New York: HarperOne, 2012.

———. *Simply Christian: Why Christianity Makes Sense*. San Francisco: HarperOne, 2010.

———. *Simply Good News: Why the Gospel Is News and What Makes It Good*. San Francisco: HarperOne, 2015.

———. *Simply Jesus: A New Vision of Who He Was, What He Did, and Why He Matters*. New York: HarperOne, 2011.

———. *Surprised by Scripture: Engaging Contemporary Issues*. San Francisco: HarperOne, 2014.

CPSIA information can be obtained
at www.ICGtesting.com
Printed in the USA
FSHW011242130121
77607FS